Acknowledgement

நவில்தொறும்நூல்நயம் போலும்பயில் தொறும்
பண்புடையாளர் தொடர்பு.

குறள் 783:

I am grateful to all local and global "peers", "well wishers" who have provided to great support and encouragement towards shaping this thesis.

I would like to thank my Guide Dr.M. Sundara Rajan Assistant professor, Department of Computer Science, Govt. Arts College, Nandanam for his great support and kind advice throughout my research studies and during the book review, it was a real privilege and an honor for me to share of his exceptional knowledge and his unrelenting support throughout this process. He has routinely gone beyond his duties to fire fight my worries, concerns, and have worked to in still great confidence in both myself and my work.

Also, I would like to thank professors who have been very supportive during my research days and through all these years. My special thanks to Dr. K. SATYANARAYANA PRINCIPAL, Sindhi College, Chennai, Dr.P.V. Kumaraguru Dy. Director; Head MCA department Gurunanak College, Velacherry Chennai 42 and Dr.P. Mayilvahanan Research In-charge, VISTAS.

My special thanks to **Dr. Mrs. Grace George Chairperson, Mrs. Suja George Vice Chairperson, Dr. D. Ashalatha Principal** and fellow members of Alpha Arts and Science College for their unstinted support throughout my work.

I finish with family, where the most basic source of my life energy resides, I have an amazing family, their support has been unconditional all these years, they have given up many things for me to stay focused on my work, they have cherished with me every great moment and supported me wherever I needed it.

Thank you!

Preface

Intended Readership

This book is primarily intended to be text for the professionals who were interested in understanding the Cloud forensics is the digital forensic which contains the different process such as data collection, examination, analysis and reporting the data for protecting the privacy of information and confidentiality. Hence, the cloud forensic is described with the process of applying digital forensic on cloud environment.

Assumed Knowledge

It was assumed that computer literacy exist for the readers, It is not mandate to have advance level cloud security is expected, basic knowledge on security and forensic is desirable.

Who can Benefit?

This book can make better understanding on digital forensic also this would help for the advance and research scholars to take this up for further analysis, since most of the findings were detailed with practical solved findings, this would help further advance studies.

Authors Profile

Dr.B. Sripriya holds a Ph.D from VISTAS in Computer Science and Master in Computer Applications from Bhardhidasan University, Srirpriya has made unique contribution in to understanding the broad sweep of technical developments in computer cloud security and digital forensics. She has authored and published several articles on cloud security at various forums. She has also integral part of many discussion forums and contributed to various workshop related to cryptography and cloud forensics computing. She is currently working as Vice Principle in Alpha Arts and Science College, Chennai.

Abstract

Cloud computing is a technology paradigm which essentially employs different computing resources. As many started storing their sensitive personal data in the cloud, security aspect of these sensitive data and their demand as well moves up steadily. Through forensic investigation, achieving security for data is an important factor while performing computing services on cloud environment.

In cloud computing, forensic investigation is introduced as a digital forensic procedure in order to identify the malicious user who initiates the crime event. This research work is focused on forensic investigation to ensure secured services over a cloud environment by analyzing and protecting the cloud log files of multiple cloud users from malicious users.

In cloud environment, many research works concentrated to perform the cloud services in a secured manner. The existing Secure-Logging-as-a-Service (SecLaaS) scheme was implemented with the objective of providing improved confidentiality and integrity entities. Through the SecLaaS scheme, generated logs protected to analysis the activity of virtual machines running in cloud. However, SecLaaS scheme failed to reduce the investigation time for discovering the malicious users while performing the forensic investigation on cloud environment.

The Forensic Acquisition and Analysis System (FAAS) were developed with the aim of better results while analyzing and acquiring the forensic data from cloud server. As per analysis it was found that FAAS not an efficient approach to ensure the log files of a real suspect while providing the user privacy. Forensic Open-Stack Tools (FROST) was presented with the objective of performing the forensic investigation by analyzing the design and implementation of management plane of forensic toolkit in an OpenStack cloud platform. However, FROST had limitations to address the issues correlated with other phases.

Existing secure provenance scheme was implemented with the aim of ensuring better confidentiality while storing a data documents on cloud environment. As the secure provenance scheme failed to perform an investigation for minimizing the cloud owner's computation overhead, Security as a service model was implemented with the aim of protecting the cloud infrastructure by providing the baseline security to provider. However, As Security as a service model had limitation in addressing security and compliance issues related with cloud infrastructures.

In order to overcome limitation of existing techniques and to ensure better secured cloud services three techniques were proposed are implemented At first, Spatio-Temporal Forensic Data Collector and Logging Filter (STFDC-LF) technique is introduced with the objective of detecting the evidence of malicious activities by using activity logs. In proposed STFDC-LF technique, Spatio-Temporal Forensic Data Collector scheme is introduced to collect the various log files from the different resources such as application logs, storage logs, computing logs and network logs by utilizing the information relevant with physical location and temporal information. This in turn, the investigation accuracy to detect the exact evidences of malicious user gets improved. Event Activity Time Synchronization method uses internal clock and external clocks for maintaining the cloud log files of multiple cloud user at a specific time. Thereby, the time taken by an investigator is minimized while performing the investigation to discover the evidences on malicious user.

Forensic Logging Filter (FLF) is deployed for isolating the log files (evidences) of multiple cloud users which is unrelated to the crime incident from the collected cloud log files and further privacy is assured with improved filtering efficiency.

Gene Optimized Multi-objective Proof Accumulator (GOMOPA) technique is introduced with the aim of identifying the malicious user by analyzing the multi-objective functions of cloud log files (evidences). The multi-objective functions hold the information about the evidence of the malicious activity, proof of integrity, provenance information, proof of data possession, time stamp information and location information. The forensic investigator reports these multi-objective functions are reported to the proof accumulator. After that, the gene based approach optimizes the multi-objective functions of cloud log files to detect the malicious user who launches the crime actions on cloud by validating the investigated proof with real suspect through the cloud service provider. Malicious user is detected on cloud environment which guarantees the confidentiality with minimal processing time.

Spatiotemporal Forensic Data Collector and Swarm Optimized Multi-Objective Proof Accumulator (SFDC-SOMOPA) technique is introduced with the objective of providing cloud services with better confidentiality rate in a secured manner. Initially, the Spatiotemporal Forensic Data Collector acquires the cloud log files of multiple cloud users from various cloud resources related with physical location and the temporal information. Thereby, the investigation accuracy is improved with the help of Spatiotemporal Forensic Data Collector. Here, Fault tolerant Time Synchronization method detects the exact time to identify the evidences of malicious activities which also reduces the investigation time.

Secondly, the Watershed Forensic Logging Filter (WFLF) performs the isolation process to separate the log files (evidences) of the multiple cloud users which are related or unrelated to the crime event from the acquired cloud log files. This in turns, the efficiency for filtering the cloud log files gets improved with the aid of WFLF. Finally, the Swarm Optimized Multi-objective Proof Accumulator (SOMOPA) is used for reporting the evidence with multi objective functions into proof accumulator. Through the particle swarm optimization, the exact malicious user who causes crime event is identified depends on the fitness calculation. Through the SFDC-SOMOPA technique, the confidentiality with minimized processing time is ensured while performing the investigation by protecting the cloud log files of normal user from malicious user.

The proposed techniques such as as Spatio-Temporal Forensic Data Collector and Logging filter (STFDC-LF), Gene Optimized Multi-objective Proof Accumulator (GOMOPA) and Spatiotemporal Forensic Data Collector and Swarm Optimized Multi-objective Proof Accumulator (SFDC-SOMOPA) techniques are implemented by using java language with CloudSim network. In order to find out the malicious user on cloud environment, the STFDC-LF technique and GOMOPA techniques utilizes Amazon EC2 dataset and SFDC-SOMOPA technique uses Amazon access sample dataset. In order to carry out the experiments, the three proposed methods are compared with existing method as Secure-Logging-as-a-Service (SecLaaS) Scheme by Shams Zawoad et al., (2016), Forensic Open-Stack Tools (FROST) by Josiah Dykstra and Alan T. Sherman (2013) and Security as a Service Model by Vijay Varadharajan and Udaya Tupakula (2014).

From the experimental results, it is evident that, the proposed SFDC-SOMOPA technique ensures better results on the parameters such as investigation accuracy, investigation time, filtering efficiency, confidentiality rate and processing time than the other proposed techniques and existing methods. With the help of Amazon access sample dataset, the investigation accuracy and filtering accuracy is improved up to 27% and 30% in the proposed SFDC-SOMOPA technique. In addition, the proposed SFDC-SOMOPA technique enhances the confidentiality rate up to 28% by using Amazon access sample dataset. Similarly, Amazon access sample dataset minimizes the investigation time and processing time by 49% and 37% in the proposed SFDC-SOMOPA technique than the other proposed and existing methods.

Table of Content

List of Tables

List of Figures

List of Abbreviation and Symbols

ABBREVIATIONS	DESCRIPTION
ABS	Attribute-based Signature Technique
API	Application Programming Interface
APT	Advanced Persistent Threat
ARM	Adaptive Resource Management
AWS	Amazon Web Service
CC	Cloud Controller
CLF	Cloud Log Forensics
C-NFMS	Current Network Forensics Methods
CSP	Cloud Service Provider
FAAS	Forensic Acquisition and Analysis System
FLF	Forensic Logging Filter
FMP	Forensic Monitoring Plane
FROST	Forensic Open-Stack Tools
FVM	Forensic Virtual Machine
GOMOPA	Multi-objective Proof Accumulator
HBST	Host Based Security Tools
HDFS	Hadoop distributed file system
IaaS	Infrastructure as a Service
LC	Log Chain
MCC	Mobile cloud computing
MHT	Merkle Hash Tree
NC	Node Controller
NFFs	Network Forensic Frameworks
NGS	Next Generation Sequencing
NLP	Natural Language processing
NTP	Network Time Protocol
PaaS	Platform as a Service
PDP	Provable Data Possession
PPL	Proof of Past Log
PSO	Particle Swarm Optimization
SaaS	Software as a Service
SCARF	SCAlable Realtime Forensics

SecLaaS	Secure-Logging-as-a-Service
SFDC-SOMOPA	Spatiotemporal Forensic Data Collector and Swarm Optimized Multi-Objective Proof Accumulator
SIEM	security Information and Event Management
SLA	Service Level Agreement
SOMOPA	Swarm Optimized Multi-objective Proof Accumulator
SPAD	Service Provider Attack Detection
STFDC-LF	Spatio-Temporal Forensic Data Collector and Logging filter
TCB	Trusted Computing Base
TPA	Third Party Auditor
TSAD	Tenant Specific Attack Detection
UTC	Universal Coordinated Time
UTM	Unified Threat Management
VDI	virtual Desktop Infrastructure
VM	Virtual Machine
WFLF	Watershed Forensic Logging Filter
'L'	Location
'CU_i'	Cloud User
W_o	Initial Weighted Vector of the Cloud Users
V_i	Temporal and Spatial Uncorrelated Data
W_l^G	Global Weighted Vector
μ	Positive Step Size
$W_{i,l}^N$	Updated Weight Vector
D_i^N	data with multiple users
u_i^T	users login time
'r'	Pearson correlation coefficient
$Sign_{PK}$	Private Key of the CSP
'd_i'	Two Events of Tenants
P_i^k	Position of Particle
V_i^{k+1}	Adjusted velocity
W_t	Weight Factor

CHAPTER I

1. Introduction

Cloud computing allows software application and services to be more robust and resilient by offering multiple layers of protection. Many organizations leverage the cloud computing benefits and as it proves to be relatively more cost-efficient compared to running conventional servers, Which means practically everything runs on the cloud these days. On the other side, increase of data being stored in the cloud increases the attack surface of cloud clusters. So high focus on cloud security and forensics is on demand. Cloud Forensics is the process of using digital forensics procedures in cloud environment. The large range of cloud forensic investigation provides various results on collecting evidence in different cloud deployment models. Digital forensic is used to report the collected and isolated data in cloud infrastructure while preserving the privacy and confidentiality of information. The Cloud forensics process performs on computer and network forensics. Cloud forensics includes the learning, analysis and reporting of information regarding the events and criminal activities. Cloud computing includes important challenges for reliable digital-forensic investigations because of several major issues. Several techniques are used in cloud forensics, to detect the source of attack, gather evidence and provide acceptable evidence.

One of the essential characteristics of moving towards cloud is to reduce cost of IT that are driving the global trend in rapid strategic adopting of cloud computing in businesses and governments. For increasing service availability and cost-effectiveness, Cloud Service Provider (CSPs) like Amazon, Salesforce.com, and Google all include the data centers in different jurisdictions providing cloud services. Reliability in data storage becomes one key aspect of CSP in cloud environment, which includes infrastructure and data center software resources, Data stored in one data center is replicated in multiple sites to safeguard from any possible data loss. It also helps is risk dependency with a particular site in event of failure. In cloud forensic, segregations of duties, roles, ownership differ based on service models. Security and dependability of cloud infrastructure has become a raising concern.

Hackers and malware are not the only one who may target a cloud services provider. Cloud computing risks are also presented by insider threats. Malicious individuals simply misuse the authority of cloud computing and manipulate attacks from nodes/hosts inside the cloud. Law enforcement agents are unable to seize the uncertain computer/digital device for accessing to the digital evidence. In cloud, each server/host includes files from several users. The privacy of other users is offended for confiscating servers/hosts from data center.

In addition, when identifying data that belongs to a particular suspect, it is difficult to separate it from other users' data. As a result, the reliability of the evidence remained uncertain.

1.1. Cloud Forensics

Cloud computing are the high scalable infrastructure resources, pay-per-use service, and low-cost on-demand computing. An interaction between multiple tenants sharing same cloud resources is not same in different deployment models. Multi-jurisdiction and multi-tenancy are employed as the common settings for cloud forensics. Cloud forensics is described by Manuel Jesús Rivas Sández (2015) as the application of digital forensics in cloud computing as subset of network forensics as shown in figure 1.1.

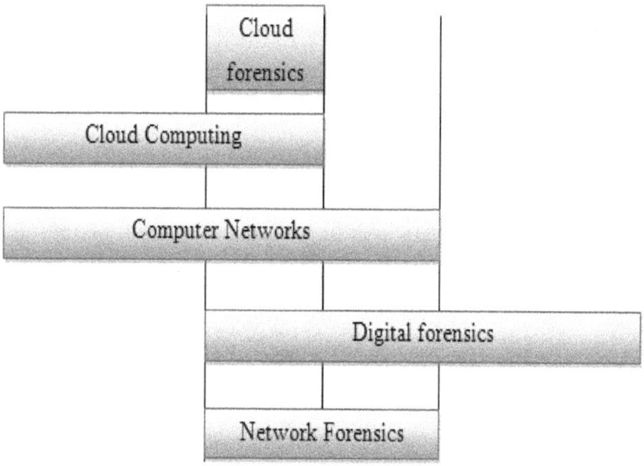

Figure 1.1: Cloud Forensics Diagram

Figure 1.1 explains where does cloud forensic lies. Digital forensics includes the investigation done at computer level for evidence of any crime that occurred by computer digital medium. Digital Forensic by Agreeka Saxen et al. (2012) categorizes the applied process in forensic carried out using digital devices that run over operating system. Digital Forensic includes computer forensics, intrusion forensics and network forensics. The essential factor of computer forensic is to retrieve the data along with the guideline and process to generate legal audit. The legal audit is to be presentable in court and to be efficiently acceptable. The aim of intrusion forensic is to identify the intrusion attack or suspicious attack of malicious user. The intrusion forensic includes any doubt-able attack against the forensic system.

Network forensic refer any natural source evidence to the crime and criminals through which crime are studied. It includes the keeping track of network accessing factor.

Mobile Forensic refers to crime being linked through the mobile phones as their medium. When the users of mobile phones are higher, maximum crime is conducted through it. Cloud computing technique includes the computer forensic along with advancement of intrusion network forensic. Computer forensic are termed as the information that act as proof to determine crime features evidence through digital medium. Digital medium are replaced by the computer medium.

The complicated collaboration between CSP and customer or multiple tenants sharing same resources are essential in many cloud forensics cases. For analyzing the problem and for emphasizing the fact that cloud forensics is a multi-dimensional problem, cloud forensics process gets expanded with three dimensions, namely organizational, legal and technical as shown in figure 1.2.

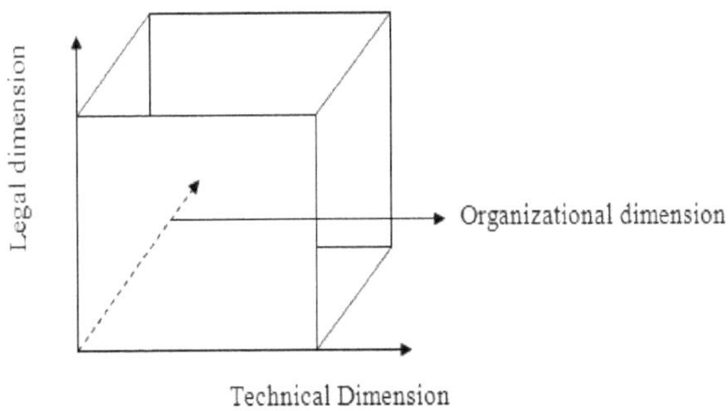

Figure 1.2: Cloud Forensic Three-Dimensional Model

From figure 1.2, the technical dimension includes set of tools and process to perform the forensic process in cloud computing environments. For establishing the forensic capability, every cloud organization with providers and customers is essential to describe structure of internal staffing, provider-customer teamwork and external support. Regulations and agreements are developed in legal dimension of cloud forensics to secure forensic activities. A design of cloud based Security Center for network security forensic analysis is carried out by Zhen Chen et al. (2013). Cloud storage maintains collected data traffic and process with cloud computing platform to identify the malicious attacks.

The cloud forensics system developed three sources namely client system, network layer and CSPs management server to gather the evidence. The cloud evidences are given by image of Virtual Machines (VMs), cloud storage files and logs. Gathering of evidence and logs from the CSP is difficult one as the cloud users and investigators have limited control over cloud infrastructure. Forensic security for digital multimedia data is examined as capable model to avoid the cyber crime activities in cloud data service provisioning. Forensic security for digital multimedia data is recognized as promising model to address the cyber crime activities in cloud data service provisioning.

In all combinations of cloud service, the cloud customer faces the demands of decreased access to forensic data. Forensic data access changes based on the cloud model. IaaS customers access to all data needed for forensic investigation while SaaS customers failed to access the necessary data. Minimal number of access to the forensic data means cloud customer has no control or knowledge over exact physical location of their data. The process is used to identify the location at higher level of abstraction as object or container identified. CSPs hide data location from the customers to assist the data movement and replication. There is a lack of suitable terms in Service Level Agreement (SLA) to allow the forensic readiness in Cloud. Software as a Service (SaaS) provider's not present access to IP logs of clients accessing content. Infrastructure as a Service (IaaS) providers failed to provide the forensic data like Virtual Machine (VM) and disk images. In Cloud, the customers decreased access to the important log files and metadata in all levels to audit the operations of network with CSP and perform real-time monitoring on own networks.

1.1.1. Digital Forensics

Digital forensics (computer forensics) is the use of scientific methods for identification, preservation, extraction and documentation of digital evidence derived from digital sources to enable successful action. The aim of digital forensics is to improve and obtain legal evidence in digital media. The current NIST definition of digital forensics is the methodical process to identify, categorize, gather, calculate and examine the data while preserving the level of integrity of information throughout the forensics process. The aim of digital forensics is forensic computing, forensic calculations and computer forensics. Judicial proceedings are one of the digital forensics problems. It required correct process in performing the forensic investigation and performing inspection setup where process or methodology depends on the scientific principles. It is essential to have proper handling of evidence to minimize the errors in investigation by digital forensic process. For trustworthiness of evidence, the digital forensic investigators are requested to explain the process in gathering evidence in a court of law.

Digital forensic investigator identifies the digital forensic process and the appropriate toolsets used for digital forensic investigation.

In conventional digital forensics, examiners hold physical access and the entire management on the evidence (process logs, router logs and hard disks). In cloud digital forensics, the control over data divides in many service models. The control of user data has three different service models (i.e. Infrastructure as a Service (IaaS), Platform as a Service (PaaS), and Software as a Service (SaaS)). Cloud user's holds maximum control in IaaS and least control in SaaS. The need of physical access of the evidence and reduction of control over the system with evidence acquisition is a significant task in the cloud environment. In cloud computing environment, the source of the evidence is ubiquitously and the correlation to the source is difficult. Besides, the investigators encompass to appoint others (inside/outside the area). The process of copying a file from one database to another and extracting the evidence in cloud storage is difficult. It consumes large amount of time and money in parallel to the investigation time. Investigators establish the computational structure, attribution of data and reliability of data. In addition, investigators preserve the stability of evidence and present/visualize it.

Cloud forensic data collection is the process of identifying, labeling, recording, and acquiring the forensic data from feasible sources of data in Cloud. The data sources comprise the client-side artifacts that exist in client ideas and provider-side artifacts exist in provider infrastructure. Segregation of duties is not same in different cloud service technique, tools and process to gather forensic data. In different models, provider-side artifacts are not same, provider-side artifacts are segregated between multiple tenants while in private clouds, there is no need. The sequence order where the data collected is described consistent with the volatility of data. The lower volatile data is collected after collecting the high volatile data. The collection process follow the process that preserve the integrity of data with segregation of duties between client and provider without breaching law and regulation under authority where the data is gathered or compromising confidentiality of any other tenants sharing the same resources.

Forensic Open-Stack Tools (FROST) by Josiah Dykstra and Alan T. Sherman (2013) presented the forensic capabilities with OpenStack in any Infrastructure-as-a-Service (IaaS) cloud platform. Cloud computing are provisioned and released with lesser attempt or service provider interaction. The forensic extensions are employed in efficient, trustworthy and user driven incident response manner.

An integrated conceptual digital forensic framework introduced by Ben Martini and Kim-Kwang Raymond Choo (2012) stressed the variations in preservation of forensic data and collection of cloud computing data for forensic purposes.

1.2. Cloud Forensic Investigation

Cloud computing uses virtualization technology on its infrastructure together with other computing services and resources provided over internet. Forensics issues in cloud computing improves the threats that needs to be reduced for achieving dependable, safe and secure cloud environment. Suchana Datta et al. (2016) explained the Cloud Forensics investigation steps for client side, server side, and developer side as described in figure 1.3.

Figure 1.3 explains four essential steps for forensic investigation in cloud. In first step, the purpose of the forensic needs is identified. After identification of forensic needs, types of cloud services are classified. In next step, the type of background technology is identified. In the fourth step, the process gets changed for client, server and developer. For client side, the user tasks are identified and activities are collected through live forensic tools. For server side, it communicates with CSP for evidence protection.

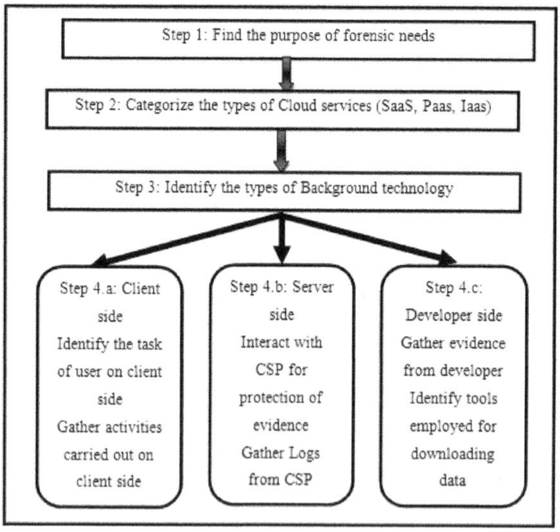

Figure 1.3: Four Steps For Forensic Investigation In Cloud Environments

Logs gathered from CSP. The evidences are gathered from developers and identify the tools used for downloading. Finally, it identifies the time consistency with the cloud service.

1.3. Process of Cloud Forensics Investigation

The cloud forensics investigation process comprises five stages. In first stage, the malicious activities are identified when any individual or CSP authority places complaints against undesirable problems. In second stage, the cloud computing generates important concerns in the cloud forensic investigation as detection and collection of appropriate malicious users.

This helps to collect and investigate the evidential artifacts since cloud data storage and the heterogeneous environment has huge development. Examinations suggest the work for involving the large number of collected data using different computerized and manual methods. The next stage is to analyze the solutions of the examination through authorization acceptable methods for attaining useful information.

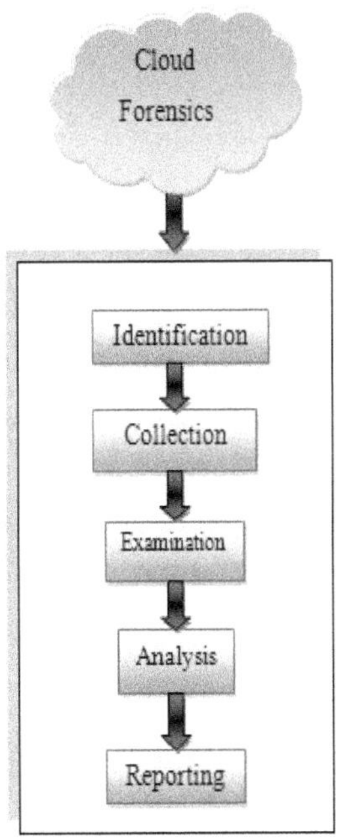

Figure 1.4: Cloud Forensics Investigation Process

During this process log files isolated which are unrelated to the crime incident. In the process of collecting evidence, the cloud forensic examiner reports the evidence of the malicious activity and also gives the proof of integrity.

In cloud forensic investigation, reporting is concerned with the submission of collected evidence to the court of law. Figure 1.4 shows the steps involved in cloud forensics investigation.

The process or steps involved for cloud forensic investigation are clearly described in below sub-section.

1.3.1. Identification

In identification phase, reporting against the malicious activities is measured as the identification that arises when any individual or CSP authority places complaints against undesirable problems. The phase includes two types of identification, namely Incident Identification and Evidence Identification.

1.3.2. Collection & Preservation

The traditional digital forensics process addresses many issues because of distributed architecture of cloud. The physical acquisition of investigation related data in many case investigators are dependent on CSPs.

Their dependence does not guarantee 100% availability of resources after collection of data. The storage capacity of collecting device is an essential problem as no data is placed in single location.

1.3.3. Examination

After collecting required number of data with CSPs, the processing is carried out by combination of manual and automation. The aim of examining is to remove and assess the data of particular classified incident scene. The integrity is preserved through whole process.

1.3.4. Analysis

The whole relevant data are examined by suitable and legally justified methods in order that suitable suspected hosts or data are identified through investigation process. Investigators addressed all queries raised in presentation of analyzed report to the court.

1.3.5. Reporting & Presentation

Reporting and Presentation are last stages of investigation process. Report includes all details of investigation process (clarification against what, why and how).

The detail report is presented to authority section with authenticity and accuracy without evidence interference of the investigation.

1.4. Forensic Acquisition and Analysis System

Cloud computing is a called as emerging computing paradigm that provides important financial advantages to business and public entities. Cloud computing provides the accessibility, integrity and portability for its customers. Due to the different combination of aspects in cloud computing that provides (including on-demand self-service, wide network access, resource pooling, fast flexibility and measured service), digital investigations face various technical, legal, and organizational demands. There are huge problems that need to be solved to perform an appropriate digital investigation in the cloud environment.

1.4.1. Forensic Acquisition and Analysis System for IaaS

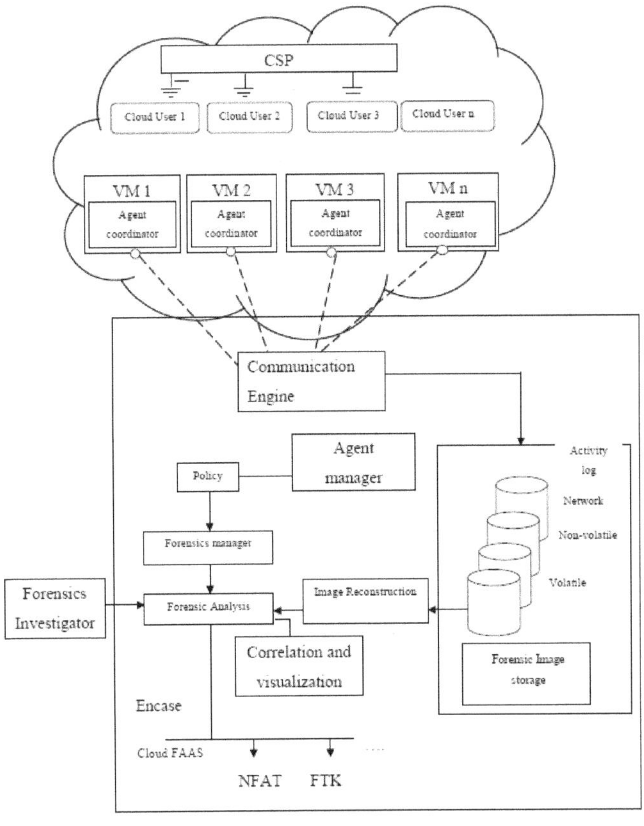

Figure 1.5: Data Acquisition Within an IaaS

Forensic acquisition and analysis system (FAAS) approach was introduced by Saad Alqahtany et al. (2016) to skip the participation of CSP while handing over control of forensic acquisition process to cloud customer by agent-based approach.

Agent-based approach is held in each VM and sending required information to central Cloud Forensic Acquisition and Analysis System (Cloud FAAS). By means of agent-based acquisition, all cloud-management data are recorded and needed for lower level data that are accessible through CSP. An innovative approach allows an image to get recreated of VM ard drive at any point in time and guarantees that every file is accessible in its entirety. Two essential factors, namely agent coordinator and Cloud FAAS are described in figure 1.5.

The agent coordinator handles agents installed inside individual VM system while Cloud FAAS is central processing point for forensic data. The agent coordinator holds the responsibility for different forms of acquisition. An acquisition policy explained by cloud customer is housed within the Cloud FAAS. There is request to enable or disable that are attained by different agents. Non-volatile memory agent is used for logically imaging the hard drive with VM. Volatile memory agent is used for logically imaging the live memory of VM. In addition, traffic agent is employed for logging and storing the network traffic. Activity log agent is an acquire system and application logs.

With nature/responsibility of VM, organizational requirements dictate the agent used. The network traffic agent is working on web front-end system as back-end server communicates with web server. The activity log agent is expected to be least used as the information generated from additional agents. The key aim is to provide the high-level log information to an investigator where overhead and cost of operating other agents is not considered. Cloud FAAS Forensic acquisition policies for VMs are described through the access provided to management information. In addition, the policies influence its effectiveness and budgetary implications. Cloud FAAS Forensic acquisition is an essential component of designed approach. It is flexible and set of standard templates are adjusted to suit organizational risk assessment. It is developed with user depending on the standard templates derived from server positions. The critical systems observe all changes across all agents while less critical systems integrate a less granular acquisition approach. The interaction between two contributing factors is presented by communication engine for the communication purpose by agent coordinator and Cloud FAAS. This communication is cryptographically secured with higher data confidentiality and integrity.

For stability of control and data integrity throughout the acquisition, agent coordinator and agent manager guarantee that the image data are hashed at all levels with complete images to files. When the task is completed, the information gets stored in forensic image storage.

The responsibility for organization with forensic manager includes providing interface to forensic investigator, ability for investigator to choose the system to get evaluated. Information is taken from image repository and image(s) reconstructed using image reconstruction module. The policy impact upon what data and extent of their granularity is to be reconstructed. Once images get reconstructed, data experiences the forensic examination and analysis.

Data collection process is a difficult process to be solved because of increasing prominence on studying the issues based on data acquisition when conducting an investigation. The process says impossibility of gaining access to the evidence in Hybrid and Public clouds is the main problem of the collecting data process.

1.5. Cloud Computing Evidence Acquisition

Digital forensic investigation is carried out with two different ways in cloud computing. In the first approach, the cloud is assumed as a tool of the crime. In the second approach, the cloud hosts a service consider as a target of the crime. In cloud environment, there are three features to be considered. Initially, the nature of crime identifies the type of the system (alive or dead) where the forensics process is performed on. Next, the current condition or appearance of cloud is established.

The availability of secure channel to collect the evidences over the cloud uses the digital signature and encryption algorithms to interact with imager device. Traditional digital forensics includes two evidence acquisitions, namely live-system/powered-on-system acquisition and dead-system/powered-off- system acquisition.

In dead system, investigators examine the hard disk images. Alive systems have the capability to examine many evidences to be acquired than the dead systems. For similar case, large amount of evidences are obtained in alive system than dead system. The relationship between both the dead and alive system are described in figure 1.5.

In cloud computing, network connection is evidence which is obtained using a live system. It is crucial to authenticate network connections to analysis the system communicates with others. Those connections include the attacker connection to compromised alive system. Network connection facilitates to reverse track criminal activities in the cloud environment.

Live systems:

- Network Connections
- Running Processes
- Memory Residence Information
- Cloud Computing Snapshots
- Security Device Logs

Dead Systems

- Hard Drive
- USB Storage
- CDs

Figure 1.6: Relationship Between Both The Dead and Alive System

Forensic investigator associates the network connections with IP addresses to analyze the results of other network security devices (e.g., Firewall, IPS). This helps to investigate the attack management that connected to the compromised system.

Business requirement of system knowledge as base, investigator knows legal installation of programs and the running process on the system. It allows the investigator to distinguish which process is usual and which one is malicious. In addition, investigator is able to acquire memory. It is considered as the huge benefits of acquiring alive system in case of encryption are deployed. This is due to the fact that encryption keys are only generated and presented in memory. In dead systems, the running memory is gone once the power is off. The evidence acquired from alive system with an virtualization is snapshots. It takes snapshots of running machine, restore and run the snapshot offline. It enables alive forensics study of snapshot involves process running, memory information and all entire connections prepared by the system.

Operating system acquisition is essential to comprehend the structure and interaction between all acquired items. Operating system in a cloud computing systems is complex than conventional one. In order to acquire operating system in cloud computing system, there are three components of the cloud system to be acquired. At first, acquire the guest operating system for determining the current back doors, system accounts which includes administrator rights and system keys. Next, acquire the host operating system (as predictor among the guest operating system/request and other cloud member operating system.) Lastly, acquire the specifications of virtualization (determine the allocated hard disk, size of memory, and network interfaces).

For big data and distributed storage, the established disk cloning is sufficient to conduct in gathering evidence in the cloud. The shared hosting is used in the cloud. The shared host includes both mistrustful material data to the cybercrime and sensitive irrelevant information. With help of naïve approach, the privacy of the irrelevant user is protected and the investigation process is enhanced by trusting the server in searching, extracting and processing the relevant data to the analyzer. In order to preserve the investigation confidentiality and security of irrelevant users in forensic investigation, many solutions are provided in cloud computing. But, the dependability and integrity of the evidence collected are not considered. The dependability and integrity are two fundamental features for admissibility of evidence in court. Therefore, encryption-then-blind signature with designated verifier scheme is used to ensure the dependability and integrity of the evidence. It is aimed to recognize the administrator in which they prove whether the collected evidence in the data comes from the server and whether the evidence is modified or not. Encryption-then-blind signature is performed based on the commutative encryption and determines its security. But, security of the method has to be still improved.

A new model for digital artifacts acquisition in cloud computing is designed by Mahmoud M. Nasreldin et al. (2015). The main objective of the concept is to ensure the secure investigation of the trusted digital evidence and show the cloud is competent to support digital forensic investigations. Besides, an encryption and digital signature algorithm is applied to ensure privacy and security for digital forensics process in the cloud environment and avoid man-in-the middle attack.

The propagation of endpoints is challenging one for data discovery and evidence gathering. The impact of crimes and workload of investigation are intensified in cloud computing due to the sheer number of resources connected to Cloud. Time synchronization is an essential to audit logs during the investigation. Exact time synchronization is an essential problem in network forensics. It is challenging as timestamps are synchronized across many physical machines in multiple geographical regions between cloud infrastructure and remote web clients with many end points.

Unification of log formats are conventional problem in network forensics and the challenge is intensified in Cloud as it is hard to combine the log formats or make them convertible to each other from huge resources in Cloud. In computer forensics, recovered deleted data is an essential source of evidence. In Amazon Web Service (AWS), the right to delete original snapshot is reserved for AWS account that generated the volume.

When attribute data are deleted in domain, removal of mapping within domain starts immediately and complete within the seconds. When the mapping is eliminated, there is no remote access to deleted data. Storage space occupied by data elements deleted is available for future write operations. Digital forensic process experiences the steps in cloud forensics with many service and deployment models.

1.6. Forensic Challenges Faced By Digital Investigators

Forensic challenges in cloud computing are examined with their recent solutions and developments by Ameer Pichan et al. (2015). Cloud forensics has many challenges because of its abstract and black box architecture. The evolutionary change improves the responsibility of cloud service provider, users, and network administrators in terms of security and privacy. Digital investigators are experiencing to address many challenges by efficient and wide-ranging forensic methodology. The key challenges facing digital investigators in investigation of MCC are given below.

1.6.1. Data Identification

Distributive and virtualized ideas had generated obstacles to digital investigators to track data in large distributed network environment. Accessibility to physical resources is an essential factor in data identification process. Resources provided by CSP are distributed in cloud and permission is required to access the data.

In addition, the level of complexity is improved and digital investigators identify and track the data during real time investigation in difficult manner because of data migration. Data identification is not feasible without the support of CSP. Digital investigators seek CSP permission by providing legal documentation that explains the requirement of the investigation.

1.6.2. Time Mismatch

A digital investigator experiences many problems regarding time synchronization of different logs at different data center. Digital evidences gathered needs to be proven in courts against intruder. It is complex and demanding problem when two different logs for the similar activity are placed at different locations with different time record.

The retrieval of many logs from different data centers generates issues such as retrieving logs from closest data center not altered while logs at distant location has more chances to be changed by intruders. Time mismatch of many logs distributed in data centers of cloud is challenging one for digital investigators.

1.6.3. *Multi-tenancy*

Many cloud users divides single object for its execution at single resource that are varied by intruder at any time. Multi-tenancy is a difficult problem for digital investigators to identify the intruder's behavior on resource by many users.

Multi-tenancy is discriminated services which is not same as other environments. Multi-tenancy includes more complexity in recognizing the intruder's data at a resource employed by more than one user simultaneously.

1.6.4. *Owner of Data*

Service level agreements (SLA) explain contract between the user and cloud service provider (CSP). In IaaS cloud service model, users include control over resources and use it based on their requirement. CSP includes the agreement with their users concerning the given resources.

It limits a digital investigator access to resources because of SLA. CSP allocates digital investigator access to resources and it is probable that particular resources are allocated to additional users as per contract ends. In addition, it generates problems to digital investigators in validating the ownership of data.

1.6.5. *Live Forensics*

Live forensics is carried out in real time network traffic flow where data is volatile. High speed data flow networks needs strong devices that collect and store network traffic. It is not probable to gather the network traffic at its time flow because of inaccessibility.

The whole network in cloud belongs to CSP and digital investigators not access to the network. A trusting relationship with CSP is essential to combine live forensics plan to collect the real time network traffic flows. Live forensics is a demanding problem because of distributed networks, high speed data flow, different network devices and different format of the data.

1.6.6. *Privacy*

Privacy is taken as main demand for digital investigator. The data of user is stored on cloud and transferred to an additional cloud under various CSP authorities.

Many users store data on cloud because of its provision on privacy. User data are analyzed and accessed by CSP where the trust value gets reduced between CSPs and users. CSP sign an agreement with clients to provide the privacy for their data.

1.6.7. Multiple Cloud Service Providers

Multiple CSPs are used by single user simultaneously. User data are stored in many clouds due to the resource constraints. Data migration is carried out in terms of entire data or some part of data sent to other cloud. Legal permission is needed to retrieve the part of data from other cloud. It is highly possible that data are changed by intruders at remote cloud data center. Digital investigators addressed the geographical, technical, and legal issues to attain multiple CSPs resources.

1.7. Problem Definition

A secure-Logging-as-a-Service (SecLaaS) was designed to protect different logs created for actions of virtual machines running in clouds and assures the confidentiality and integrity of logs. But, the cloud forensic investigation time was not minimized in cloud infrastructure. An efficient forensic acquisition and analysis system (FAAS) was introduced in Infrastructure as a Service model. But, it failed to attain the log files of a real suspect while guaranteeing the user privacy.

A technical and trust issues were taken place in gathering the forensic evidence discovered from infrastructure-as-a-service cloud computing and observes many approach for addressing the threats. But, it failed to determine the legal difficulties of acquisition. Forensic challenges in cloud computing examines new solutions and developments. But, the development of solutions and standard possibility were not taken.

A Forensic Open-Stack Tools (FROST) was designed in a data acquisition phase and other phases of process affected by cloud computing remained unaddressed. An incorporated conceptual digital forensic approach was designed based on McKemmish and NIST. But, it failed to authenticate the evidence created by integrated approach. A distributed data store was designed that utilize the object model to store and to retrieve the forensic data. But, the space complexity remained unaddressed.

Security as a service model was introduced for providing the baseline security to provider for preserving its own cloud infrastructure and provides the flexibility to tenants. But, the cloud infrastructures suffer from number of security and compliance problems. A new secure provenance scheme was introduced based on group signature and attribute-based signature process. But, an efficient investigation was not carried out to minimize the cloud owner's computation overhead. A digital forensic investigation was performed for gathering the data by agent established on cooperation system in cloud. However, the exact evidence was not attained with high priority.

1.8. Proposal Work

Initially, to collect and isolate evidence with activity logs in cloud, Spatio-temporal Forensic Data Collector and Logging filter (STFDC-LF) technique is designed. STFDC-LF technique identifies evidence of malicious user using forensic logging filter. STFDC-LF technique retrieves cloud log files of Virtual machine (VM) resource with evidence against malicious activity. Spatio-temporal Forensic Data Collector collects the cloud log files from cloud resources like application logs, storage logs, computing logs, and network logs by developing the information related to physical location and temporal information.

Event Activity Time Synchronization method is introduced across collected log files of particular crime incident. Forensic Logging Filter (FLF) isolates log files of many cloud users by correlation measure with probabilistic structure while guaranteeing data privacy of malicious users and cloud users. This designed technique minimizes the diversity of log files depending on crime time, location and guaranteeing the privacy preservation of logs in target VM.Next, to report the evidence and to prove crime activities in cloud, a Gene Optimized Multi-objective Proof Accumulator (GOMOPA) technique is presented. GOMOPA technique helps to report collected and isolated data to accumulator for identifying malicious user. In GOMOPA technique, cloud forensic investigator submits evidence of malicious activity, proof of integrity, provenance information, proof of data possession, time stamp information and location information to multi-objective proof accumulator. Multi-objective functions are optimized by means of gene based approach. GOMOPA technique identifies the malicious user by verifying the investigated evidence with real suspect by Cloud Service Provider (CSP). GOMOPA technique identifies suspect who initiates malicious activities over cloud infrastructure. This designed technique increases the confidentiality of cloud users' log files and preserving many cloud users who are malicious users.

Finally, an integration of Spatiotemporal Forensic Data Collector and Swarm Optimized Multi-objective Proof Accumulator (SFDC-SOMOPA) technique is designed. SFDC-SOMOPA technique includes three processes to identify malicious user with admissible evidence. Spatiotemporal Forensic Data Collector gathers the number of cloud log files from different cloud resources with physical location and temporal information. Fault tolerant Time Synchronization method applied across collected log files extract the precise time and increases the reliability for identifying the malicious event. Watershed Forensic Logging Filter (WFLF) isolates crime log files of multiple cloud users for data privacy.

Swarm Optimized Multi-objective Proof Accumulator (SOMOPA) reports evidence with multi objective functions to identify correct malicious user through fitness calculation. SFDC-SOMOPA technique identifies real suspect who launches malicious activities over cloud infrastructure with higher the confidentiality of the cloud users' log files.

1.9. Organization of the Thesis

The research is organized as follows:

Chapter 1 designs the primary problems and challenges faced while identifying the malicious user with admissible evidence through cloud forensic investigation in cloud computing.

Chapter 2 reviews the previous work done in cloud computing, data investigation techniques in cloud forensics, identification of malicious attacks, forensics analysis techniques, fault tolerance techniques in cloud forensics and so on.

Chapter 3 explains an effective Spatio-temporal Forensic Data Collector and Logging filter (STFDC-LF) technique for collecting and isolating the evidential artifacts with activity logs in cloud.

The main aim of STFDC-LF technique is to minimize the diversity of log files depending on crime time, location and guaranteeing the privacy preservation of logs in target VM.

Chapter 4 describes an effective Gene Optimized Multi-objective Proof Accumulator (GOMOPA) technique to report the evidence and prove crime activities in cloud. The main of aim of GOMOPA technique helps to report collected and isolated data to accumulator for identifying malicious user.

Chapter 5 elaborates an effective Spatiotemporal Forensic Data Collector and Swarm Optimized Multi-objective Proof Accumulator (SFDC-SOMOPA) technique to identify malicious user with admissible evidence.

The main objective of proposed SFDC-SOMOPA technique identifies real suspect who launches malicious activities over cloud infrastructure with higher the confidentiality of the cloud users' log files.

Chapter 6 explains the result analysis on STFDC-LF technique, GOMOPA scheme and SFDC-SOMOPA Technique in terms of investigation accuracy, investigation time, processing time, confidentiality rate and filtering efficiency and so on.

The final **Chapter 7** summarizes the key results, conclusions of this thesis and outlines potential future work.

1.10. Summary

Cloud forensic investigation helps in identifying the malicious user with admissible evidence. It gives an introduction abut the process of cloud forensic investigation and challenges for digital forensics in cloud computing. Also, many techniques are described for addressing the cloud forensic investigation issues in brief manner. Furthermore, the literature survey, proposal work and the organization of the thesis is presented.

CHAPTER II

LITERATURE REVIEW

2.1. Introduction

Cloud computing, technology that enables the users to upload data to the web, permits for direct accessibility and the capability to distribute data with others at any time Cloud computing is a way of computing which is dynamically expandable and presents essential resources for service provider via internet. Cloud computing is a truly mobile workforce when compared to yesteryears of computing; As long as there is a internet connectivity anyone can access the data from any locations. It also brings a great financial savings through custom made packages which provide privacy, integrity, confidentiality and security to the available data by vendors around the world. Efficiency and Cost utilization makes the cloud computing more popular and significant.

In cloud technology, with help of internet the data is easily uploaded and distributed from one computer to another without exiting a huge amount of observable evidence. As a result, it challenges the forensic investigators. The function of digital forensics in cloud computing is named as cloud forensics. Cloud forensics is considered as an intermediate discipline among the cloud computing and digital forensics. Cloud forensics is one of the rising fields in cloud computing which helps in recognizing the digital crime occurred over the cloud. The crime investigators involved in the cloud environment maintains the evidence which resides anywhere for identifying the malicious attacks. Usually 3rd parties are associated with cloud service providers, due to this possibility of malicious actions or event might occur in stored cloud data. In spite of availability of various techniques to protect data from malicious actions, cloud forensics facing many challenges in preserving the information with high security and confidentiality. So it is therefore number of literature papers were analyzed and examined for enhancing performance of cloud forensic investigation.

2.2. Digital Forensic Investigation Techniques

Raymond Lutui (2016) introduced multidisciplinary digital forensic investigation system. Multidisciplinary digital forensic investigation process model was a superior process model for improving the value and proficiency of investigation in multidisciplinary environment. The straw man model was analyzed and examined for detecting the necessary requirements. This resulted in invention of multidisciplinary digital forensic investigation process model.

Multidisciplinary digital forensic investigation process model increased the possibility of investigation process in cloud forensics. But multidisciplinary digital forensic investigation process model enhanced the investigation time.

The most difficult challenge in cloud computing was digital forensic investigation because of the complex architecture of cloud environment. The data in the complex architecture of cloud is coordinated and retrieved through several devices and it minimizes the identification of real device to grasp for forensic investigation. Ghania Al Sadi (2015) investigated the cloud architecture complexity and digital inquiries of cloud forensics. However the analysis could not address the malicious attacks during the investigation (forensic).

M. Taylor et al. (2010) analyzed the official characteristic of digital forensic investigations of cloud computing systems. Distributed processing of digital data was provided by cloud computing. The digital evidence acquisition and examination was made more challenging due to systems involved in digital forensic investigation. Some of the evidence was present in different jurisdictions and certain organizations encrypt the evidence before it was being delivered to the forensic investigators. Delay was increased in the investigation process. In digital evidence examination, all the malicious actions happened in the digital forensics of cloud computing was analyzed and studied. However, confidentiality rate of data remains unconsidered.

Farhood Norouzizadeh Dezfoli et al. (2013) considered cloud forensic application and security issues. Digital forensic is the process of investigating the computer crimes. The traditional techniques involved in data collection and processing in cloud forensic was examined and studied. In addition to, the illegal issues of cloud forensic were observed for enhancing the performance of cloud forensics but investigation accuracy remains unaddressed.

Ezz El-Din Hemdan and Manjaiah D.H (2015) presented a forensic analysis approach for digital objects namely digital photos and documents. In the forensic analysis approach, vital metadata was offered which were utilized for investigating crimes in the cloud by the cloud investigators. The attackers also utilized the metadata for implementing illegal activities that helped the investigators to easily perform forensic investigation because of provision of consistent information. At first, metadata was produced from documents and digital photos. Then, hash values were generated by hash algorithm to enhance the integrity of data in cloud services. The produced hash values and metadata were kept for forensic investigation in local storage.

In case of any illegal activity performed in the cloud storage data from malicious users, then the investigators were allowed to access these hash values kept in the local storage. The data integrity was also verified but failed to enhance the filtering efficiency.

R.B. van Baar et al. (2014) designed digital forensic process. The digital forensic process was applied to the present and traditional digital forensic process and examined the factors influencing the efficiency of its process. Traditional digital forensic process was optimized and served better in identifying the malicious attacks. However, the investigation time was increased in digital forensic process.

Deoyani Shirkhedkar and Sulabha Patil (2014) analyzed digital forensic challenges and issues. The maintenance of security in cloud computing is a challenging task. Malicious attacks occur due to the absence of security mechanisms in cloud. Flexible accessing of cloud computing without physical infrastructures makes more suitable for malicious users. The problems faced by forensic investigators in collecting evidence left by the degraded performance were examined but the filtering efficiency remains unaddressed.

2.3. Data Investigation Techniques in Cloud Forensics

Shams Zawoad et al. (2016) presented Secure-Logging-as-a-Service (SecLaaS). SecLaas was utilized to control the malicious users from destroying the privacy and integrity of logging actions performed by virtual machines in cloud computing. According to SecLaas, only the investigators were allowed to contact the activity logs through RESTful API. The confidentiality rate of logs was increased. Then for enhancing the integrity of the logs, the evidence of previous logs delivered by the cloud providers and hash-chain scheme were considered. The evidence of previous logs was constructed by utilizing accumulator schemes namely Bloom filter and RSA accumulator. Bloom-Tree was employed for reducing the time and space necessities. However, the investigation accuracy was not increased by using SecLaaS.

Saad Alqahtany et al. (2016) developed forensic acquisition and analysis system (FAAS) as a Service model. The problems that have to be addressed for improving the performance of cloud forensics were specified. The result from the analysis stated that without employing cloud service providers (CSPs), it was impractical to carry out investigation and recognition in cloud environment. The investigators were dependent on CSP for attaining evidence from cloud systems. In FAAS, there was no need of any involvement or assistance from cloud provider. FAAS which was an analysis system provided better performance than present CSP but failed to reduce the investigation time.

Josiah Dykstra and Alan T. Sherman (2012) described the technical problems of trust in obtaining the forensic evidence from infrastructure-as-a-service cloud computing along with its strategic challenges. At first, a model was built to expose the trust layers in the cloud. Then, an overacting context was estimated for cloud forensic investigation and examined the examiner options. Admired forensic acquisition tool was evaluated. This exposed that popular forensic acquisition tool was able to distinguish the volatile and non-volatile cloud data. Moreover, four additional executions for acquisition-Trusted Platform Modules, the management plane, forensics-as-a-service, and legal explanation were included. These solutions minimized the trust but necessitated more support from cloud service provider. Though trust layers were avoided, the confidentiality rate of evidence was not considered.

In cloud computing, the process of digital forensics covers the isolated data, chain of custody, big data and ownership. Mahmoud M. Nasreldin et al. (2015) established digital artifacts acquirement as a combination of digital forensic and cloud computing. Through digital artifacts acquisition, a safe investigation was offered for the trusted digital evidence. Then, the Hou et al.'s scheme was observed with respect to integrity and authenticity properties. The integrity and authenticity of Hou et al.'s scheme was proved to be dissatisfied in severe-aided confidential forensics investigation. Encryption and digital signature algorithms were introduced to increase the confidentiality and chain of custody in cloud forensics. But digital artifact acquisition failed in enhancing the filtering efficiency.

Meng You et al. (2014) developed the concept of urgent data to reduce the reaction time of monitoring system. The monitoring systems were used for offering monitoring services to the cloud environment. With the aid of urgent data, the response time of urgent queries was minimized by decreasing the bandwidth utilization. The monitoring data was treated in a different way. Data which recorded the actions of critical system addresses the monitoring speed was called as urgent data. In case of critical errors, high speed urgent data group assisted the system to respond in real time. Urgent data also helped in decreasing the response latency. However, the concept of urgent data minimized the investigation accuracy.

The primary consideration of privacy and security is important in cloud forensics for a well-organized crime investigation. Muhammad Irfan et al. (2016) developed a framework utilizing security information and event management (SIEM) for cloud forensics. The main involvement of developed framework was consideration of efficient evidence group in crime investigation and also data was shared whenever the cloud user needed. In SIEM, the passive attacks were considered and offered necessary explanations from the cloud service provider.

Efficient evidence construction was also guaranteed by the developed framework for crime examination but the data investigation time was increased.

In cloud computing, privacy preservation of cloud data is a demanding task. Chu-Hsing Lin et al. (2012) described digital forensics structure for RSA signature in cloud computing. Digital forensic structure increased the privacy and employed forensic officers to preserve computing power. Through RSA signature protocol utilized in digital forensic structure, the evidences were checked by the verifier. The computing load and storage space was minimized but confidentiality rate was low by using digital forensics structures.

A number of applications are interested in the use of cloud computing for data investigation. Ben Martini and Kim-Kwang Raymond Choo (2012) described an integrated conceptual digital forensic framework in cloud forensics. Integrated conceptual digital forensic framework considered the safeguarding of forensic data and cloud computing data grouping. The criminal operations in accumulating the incriminating files in cloud computing was avoided by the digital forensic framework. Though security of data was improved, the investigation time was high in integrated conceptual digital forensic framework.

The large scale distribution of cloud storage makes file investigation more difficult in cloud forensics. GAO Yuanzhao and LI Binglong (2017) designed a forensic method depending on three-level (3L) mapping for file acquisition. With the study of Hadoop distributed file system (HDFS), forensic method was executed. In HDFS file, the 3L mapping was recognized from HDFS namespace and delivered to data block presented in local file system. Then through Xen virtualization platform, multi-node Hadoop framework was constructed for checking the performance of forensic technique. Forensic method performed better in attaining a capable location of stored files and accurately selected disk image with increased recovery of deleted files. But, HDFS decreased the data collection accuracy.

Yee-Yang Teing et al. (2017) discussed cooperative cloud storage services. Through symform, the data remnants were established with the aid of cooperative cloud storage services. A set of mobile devices and personal computers were measured. The potential artefacts in data were observed during installation and uninstallation of cloud applications with file synchronization and time stamp information. The various terrestrial artifacts occurred during the use of cooperative storage cloud on client devices was estimated and studied. However, the filtering efficiency was low in cooperative storage services.

Josiah Dykstra and Alan T. Sherman (2013) discussed three new forensic tools called FROST for OpenStack cloud platform.

FROST was utilized in maintaining an infrastructure-as-a-Service (IaaS) cloud and offered a trustworthy forensic investigation. Without interrelating with operating system, FROST functioned at the cloud management phase. This assisted in avoiding the usage of guest machine. Then, the integrity of data was protected by storing the evidence in hash trees and delivering them with the aid of cryptographic hashes. The tools employed in FROST processed the investigations without the interaction of cloud provider. Specific features of FROST allowed the investigators to acquire data from OpenStack cloud. But, FROST increased the investigation time.

The utilization of digital forensics increases the field of cloud computing. Sonal Saokar et al. (2015) developed a framework for implementing forensic in the cloud environment. Adaption of digital forensic in cloud computing is challenging due the restriction of data acquisition. The developed framework helped in constructing custom overflow on cloud data. The framework included HBase, MapReduce techniques for well-organized analysis on cloud data but reduced the confidentiality level of evidence.

The progress of cloud computing for Internet of Things (IoT) is drastically increased. The virtual desktop infrastructure (VDI) is used by various companies for minimizing the cost and enhancing the servers in private cloud computing. The reduction of malicious attacks on VDI is a challenging task. Doowon Jeong et al. (2015) developed investigation methodology for VDI solutions. In the developed investigation methodology, virtual desktop infrastructure and different desktop visualization solutions are involved namely VMware, Citrix, and Microsoft. The analysis of data integrity was carried out to prove that the investigation methodology was suitable as evidence. Even though VDI increased the data integrity, the filtering efficiency was decreased.

The network forensic investigation has to address with security related concerns. Daniel Spiekermann et al. (2017) developed Virtual Network Forensic Process which was a forensic framework. In Virtual Network Forensic Process, a forensic controller called ForCon was framed. ForCon investigated the network in OpenFlow controlled network with the aid of Open vSwitch. Then, alteration of the installed capture process was carried out by monitoring the virtual environment with dislocated agents in the network without any investigator. Flexible and suitable evidence was provided to the network forensic investigation in virtual networks but the data collection accuracy was reduced.

Christopher Stelly and Vassil Roussev (2017) designed a container-based software framework called SCAlable Realtime Forensics (SCARF).

SCARF was implemented with forensic computations. By the offering of low-cost integration of both custom code and an array of third-party tools, SCARF was virtually explained with uncomplicated data interfaces. The obtained system appears similar to the data parallel nature of forensic tasks restricting parallel implementation. Then the inclusion of hardware resources linearly increased the processing tasks namely, hashing, indexing and bulk processing-performances. However, SCARF failed in enhancing the confidentiality rate of data.

Hyunji Chung et al. (2012) initialize the process model for forensic investigation of cloud storage services. The utilization of cloud computing is extremely progressed because of the invention of large number of digital devices. Several malicious users arise for degrading the performance of cloud storage. This influences a requirement of examining the forensic investigation in cloud storage serves. The introduced process model examined and studied the malicious threats of all obtainable devices namely, Windows system, Mac system, iPhone, and Android smartphone. Though the process model improved the security, the filtering efficiency was not increased to the desired level.

Chi Yang et al. (2014) introduced spatiotemporal compression technique to address the problem of big graph data processing on cloud. In spatiotemporal compression technique, the compression of big data was executed out with respect to spatiotemporal features on cloud. Then, a graph data set was distinguished into clusters through spatial data correlation. The workload was shared by the interference on the basis of time series relationship in a cluster. After that, temporal data compression was followed by the development of temporal correlation in each single graph edge. The use of data driven scheduling helped in data processing optimization. Spatiotemporal compression and scheduling performed better in provisions of data size and data reliability loss. Although spatiotemporal compression technique minimized the data fidelity loss, the data investigation time was increased.

Yee-Yang Teing et al. (2017) analyzed an admired cloud storage service called CloudMe. The increase in the amount of data causes artefacts to the forensic investigators to have an up-to-date knowledge about the evidential big data. The collection, processing and investigations become more costly. CloudMe provides a solution to these limitations. In this analysis, the various categories of artefacts including their places along with installation and uninstallation of CloudMe client application were provided. Then, the logging in and out, actions from desktop computer to mobile clients were explained. These analyses helped in improving the performance of forensic investigation with big data but confidentiality rate of data was decreased.

2.4. Identification of Malicious Attacks

Ameer Pichan et al. (2015) analyzed the forensic challenges faced by cloud computing along with its acceptable solutions. The problems of cloud computing with conventional digital forensics phases were examined. By considering the phases of conventional digital forensics, the challenges and its acceptable solutions were listed out. As a result, the difference among the issues of non-cloud and cloud digital forensics was detected. The investigators were provided with a better recognition about the cloud environment issues. Various developments in cloud forensics were also included. Although the malicious attacks were resolved, the data security level was minimized.

Cloud forensics helps in collecting documents cloud service provider more easily. The more difficult task was to design a framework that overcomes the challenges of cloud forensics. Deevi Radha Rani et al. (2016) discussed the various challenges faced by cloud forensics with acceptable solutions. In order to solve the various challenges, an effort of collecting solutions was carried out and an effective framework was designed for cloud forensics. However, the investigation accuracy failed to improve.

Shahaf Rozanski and Cellebrite (2015) discussed the challenges faced by the investigators during the retrieval of data from the cloud. The forensic investigators are more benefited from cloud data. Cloud data sources also offer significant connections investigators with the aid of mobile device data for resolving the crime actions. This analysis portrayed all the issues and abuses in the process of data gathering for investigation. But the investigation time was not considered for better performance of cloud forensics.

Darren Quick and Kim-Kwang Raymond Choo (2013) reviewed three public cloud storage providers in the process of data acquisition and storage. The data collection and storage was carried out in Dropbox, Google Drive, and Microsoft SkyDrive by employing browser with client software. Then, the output was matched with the original files. Through the comparison, it was observed that there was no modifications occurred in the data during uploading, storage and downloading. In addition to, the timestamps of the files was also verified and it remained the same. Timestamp was considered as an essential aspect of investigation and thus the information has to be understood with respect to timestamp on a file. However, the confidentiality rate of data was not preserved.

Digital investigations include building of virtual machine (VM) computer activity timelines. Those constructed timelines are a collection of ancient traces of hypervisor kernel system logs originated on VM host computer file system.

Sean Thorpe and Indrajit Ray (2012) designed Virtual machine log auditor to address the problems of cloud computing digital investigations. Virtual machine log auditor was a software tool which identified the unpredictability within virtual machine timelines. Virtual machine log auditor helped in predicting the contact of deliberate tampering. Then, several techniques were implemented to handle the temporal variation. However, Virtual machine log auditor decreased the filtering efficiency.

Cloud log forensics (CLF) assists in detecting the malicious actions against log investigation by intense cloud analysis. The accessibility attributes inhibit the investigation of cloud logs. Suleman Khan et al. (2016) analyzed the CLF and the challenges that complicated the cloud log data investigation. Through this analysis, CLF significance, logging mode and cloud-as-a-service was highlighted. The performance of CLF in investigation of cloud log was examined which helped in detecting malicious actions. The security necessities, vulnerability and challenges of CLF were detected to manage the issues in maintaining the cloud logs but the investigation accuracy remains unaddressed.

M. Edington Alex and R. Kishore (2017) presented a model for storing forensic evidence. The challenges of cloud computing in forensic investigation were analyzed. The resulting analysis stated that cloud forensics depends on cloud service provider (CSP). The data gathered for forensic investigation was modified by CSP and the investigation process stops. The presented model helped in avoiding the dependency of CSP. The centralized forensic server and a forensic layer called forensic monitoring plane (FMP) was checked to know whether it had collected the required information about malicious attacks. But, the analysis failed to enhance the data collection accuracy.

Agreeka Saxena et al. (2012) investigated the process of cloud forensics with cloud computing. The various drawbacks and advantages of forensic investigations were also mentioned. Forensic investigation is a technique of checking the evidences. The use of cloud computing with forensics resulted in computer forensic. By the utilization of computers, the crime evidences were gathered to detect the threats occurred due to malicious actions. The security requirements of cloud forensics were also considered and protective measures were taken against those malicious behavior. But, methods were not taken for enhancing the filtering efficiency.

Himanshu Nimje and Dr K. N. Honwadkar (2015) reviewed the dedicated issues in cloud for android convenient criminology.

Then difficulty faced by cloud computing in mobile forensics and the challenges of forensic investigation in cloud computing were discussed. Although data security level was considered, the investigation time was not reduced to the desired level.

Forensic investigation is supported through the identification and investigation of data enabled by network forensics. Suleman Khan et al. (2014) described the flexibility of Network Forensic Frameworks (NFFs) on application with Mobile cloud computing (MCC). For examination, a classification was considered in recognizing the architecture of NFF with detailed description about the fundamental mechanisms. However, the issues of malicious attack were not mentioned.

Mark Taylor et al. (2011) analyzed the challenges of forensic investigation in cloud computing. The forensic investigation was more complex due to data stored at various authorities on internet-based cloud computing systems. Delay was occurred before delivering data to the investigators. Some of the organizations encrypt the data and it created more complexity with delay in acquiring the required digital evidence. Cloud forensic investigators required a huge amount of data for a better understanding and examining of evidences in cloud computer environment. Cloud computing environment also included tools, application and architecture for detecting, acquiring and examining the evidence for forensic investigation. Although, data acquisition was made better, the investigation time was increased.

Suchana Datta et al. (2016) analyzed the challenges of cloud forensics along with measures for preserving the security aspects. The provided measures also included architectures and research scopes for restricting the malicious attacks. The security level was improved but confidentiality rate of data was unaddressed.

Keyun Ruan et al. (2013) reviewed the analysis of digital forensic authorities and practitioners on cloud forensics. The important condition for recognizing the basic issues in cloud forensics including definition, scope, challenges and opportunities were examined. But, methods for increasing the investigation accuracy remains addressed.

2.5. Forensics Analysis Techniques

Flavio Cruz et al. (2015) introduced distributed data store for GRR. Distributed data store was an incident response framework in which AF4 object model was utilized for accumulating and recovering forensic data. The specific characteristics of access pattern were relieved by GRR. This amplified data processing and scalability of GRR. In distributed data store, the data was separated into database files. The independent accessing of separated database files permitted scalable manner of distributed forensic analysis.

Then, the NSRL software reference database was described which helped in restricting the resource wastage incase of file collection from enterprise machines. However, data collection time was increased in distributed data store.

Zhen Chen et al. (2013) presented collaborative network security management system. The presented management system included an efficient collaborative Unified Threat Management (UTM) and traffic probers. The UTM employed distributed security overlay network and centralized security influencing peer-to-peer communication protocol. The virtual connection of distributed security overlay network helped in exchanging network actions and security rules. At first, cloud-based security center was designed by employing cloud storage in collaborative network security management system. This examined the network security forensic and retained the gathered traffic. Then, the assembled traffic data was treated with cloud computing platforms which in turn detected the malicious attacks. Important computing and storage resources based on actual trace data were observed and the phishing attack forensic examination was carried out. Each collaborative UTM and prober for gathering the actions and traffic were initiated by the cloud based security center and according to the traffic, essential security rules were produced. The collaborative UTM imposed the produced security rule and the actions of security rules were delivered back to the security center. Collaborative network security management performed better in detecting the new distributed attacks efficiently because of its close-loop control. But, collaborative network security management system failed in addressing the confidentiality rate of data.

Rohini Patil et al. (2016) designed a system for evaluating safety measures of Android mobile apps. The system was employed to prevent the fraud apps based on cloud stack and data mining. Natural language processing (NLP) was used in designing the developed system and positive negative rating was analyzed. However, the processing time was not addressed.

G.Geethakumari and AbhaBelorkar (2012) presented fuzzy clustering techniques for discovering the presence and activities of malicious threats. The fuzzy clustering techniques helped in obtaining more reliable and efficient evidence of attacks. The resulting evidence was sequenced, incorporated utilized for qualitative examination of IDS/IPS system. Then, the time-complexity for attaining back-end calculation was reduced with higher efficiency but data collection accuracy was reduced.

Chen Long and Zhang Qing (2015) described the terrestrial artifacts found on client's machine. Then, method was established for reconstructing the user's actions.

Reconstruction was carried out by linking the various traces obtained from the client's activities and examining the user's data operation behavior for investigation. But, the investigation time was not mentioned.

2.6. Security Enhancement Techniques in Cloud Forensics

In cloud computing, enhancement of cloud users' trust is a challenging task. Adeela Waqar et al. (2013) considered a framework depends on database schema redesign and dynamic reconstruction of metadata. The considered framework was utilized in preserving the cloud user's data privacy. By utilizing cryptographic and relational privacy preservation operations, database schema was customized. Customization of database schema was carried out by sensitivity parameterization parent class membership in cloud database. Then, dynamic reconstruction of metadata guaranteed the unchanged database file accession. This helped in reformation of original database schema. However, data collection accuracy was not increased.

In cloud forensics, the maintenance of user's confidence and integrity is considered as a challenging task. Jiawei Yuan and Shucheng Yu (2015) developed integrity auditing system for cloud data distributing services. The integrity auditing scheme was differentiated into multi-user modification, public auditing, high error detection probability, capable user revocation with communication auditing performance. In integrity auditing scheme, user impersonation attack was considered and avoided. Multi-user modification was preserved and the drawbacks of traditional techniques were solved. Multiple tasks batch auditing was also improved through integrity auditing scheme but failed in considering the investigation time.

An efficient data forensics in cloud computing was attained through secure provenance. Jin Li et al. (2013) introduced secure provenance scheme depending on group signature and attribute-based signature method. Through secure provenance scheme, the cloud data was offered with confidentiality, cloud user's anonymous authentication, fine-grained access control and provenance tracing of uncertain documents. Then, computational overhead was minimized in provenance process by employing the cloud users. The required security techniques were implemented for enhancing the security concerns of the introduced provenance scheme. Though security requirements were fulfilled, the confidentiality rate of data was minimized.

Vijay Varadharajan and Udaya Tupakula (2014) discussed security architecture as a service model for countering the attacks in opposition to the customers or tenants. The discussed security architecture provided defense to its own cloud infrastructure and flexibility to the customers contain higher security functionalities in controlling the virtual machines.

Usually, every tenant has security functionalities. There were still few tenants needed to have additional security for protecting from malicious attacks. The security architecture offered security required tenants to reveal some information about its services and applications. The privacy and security of the cloud provider was enhanced. However, the security architecture failed to increase the filtering efficiency.

Zhen Xu et al. (2014) discussed hassle-free, fixed-rate and job-based software including integrity verification mechanism. Hassle-free, fixed-rate and job-based software was a service model which addressed the problem of convex optimization. The integrity verification mechanism was implemented by utilizing application-specific techniques. Then, a security design was constructed without any heavy cryptographic tools. Computation outsourcing proof-carrying attained well-organized integrity verification. Through Hassle-free, fixed-rate and job-based software, the client side was offered with significant computational savings and cloud side with marginal overhead. But hassle-free, fixed-rate and job-based software decreased the data collection accuracy.

The most difficult task in cloud computing is to check whether the available data are secured properly. Jian Shen et al. (2017) introduced public auditing protocol among global and blockless verification. Different auditing properties like blockless verification and batch auditing was also added. A doubly linked info table and location array was contained in public auditing protocol. Then, the data dynamics was protected securely with a dynamic structure. The computational and communication overhead was decreased and the efficiency was also increased but confidentiality rate remains unaddressed.

Sarah F. Bailey et al. (2017) presented a model for constructing cloud environment for forensic analysis in Next Generation Sequencing (NGS) data. At first, a complete front-to-end cloud system was implemented which uploaded, developed and interpreted the unrefined NGS data with the aid of web browser dashboard. The implemented system was expandable and analyzed autosomal and Y-STRs in terms of quality from different NGS instrumentation. For STRs, the data from NGS was concordant categorized by capillary electrophoresis and Sanger sequencing using regular reference materials. Then, the cloud computing power was estimated through on-demand autoscaling. This enables multiple file investigation in tandem. Complete front-to-end cloud system accumulated the obtained data in a relational database through the guidance of sequenced alleles nomenclature. Multi-layered cloud security architecture was constructed for protecting the NGS data from bioinformatic effects. The presented model assisted in enhancing the feasibility of NGS data for forensic investigation but failed to address the filtering efficiency.

Christian J. D'Orazio and Kim-Kwang Raymond Choo (2016) designed adversary model for increasing the security of cloud apps in forensic investigation. Mobile apps are more suspicious to threats because of the storage of sensitive data and posses more digital evidence. Forensic investigation in such devices is very significant. The adversary model restricted the security mechanisms and artefacts from cloud apps. Necessities of circumvention techniques with the aid of famous iOS cloud apps were observed. Then, iOS cloud app security taxonomy was introduced for utilization in advanced persistent threat (APT) incident investigation. Though the security was improved, the processing time was not minimized to the desired level.

Prasad Purnaye and Varshapriya Jyotinagar (2015) presented cloud model to enhance forensics in cloud with elevated security. Through the presented cloud model, the volatile data of each customer was stored. Then, para-virtual environment was built by utilizing KVM hypervisor for execution. A module was employed for gathering the volatile data and saved in determined storage of volatile data storage and recovery. Since IaaS had more degree of control, IaaS was selected. On the basis of private cloud, the virtual machines were organized. The volatile data was obtained through sharing of determined storage after the VM booting and the data was saved but confidentiality rate of data was reduced.

Roberto Battistoni et al. (2016) presents generic time model and CURE architecture for offering timeline flexibility to nodes in cloud computing. The generic time model identified the time-based exploitations and threats. The main objective of this model was to guarantee timeline integrity to the host devices. In generic time model, the trusted entity called cloud controller (CC) was not changed by an adversary. CURE offered the network with framework which was allowed to effectively detect the malicious threats in the cloud through two security aspects namely, Time Heartbeat, Anti-forging mechanisms and key management. However, CURE minimized the data collection accuracy.

The distribution of processing units, storage devices and applications were provided by cloud computing. Muhammad Naeem Ahmed Khan and Shah Wali Ullah (2017) presented an analysis model depends on aggregating accessible logs from clients and servers to identify the malicious activity on cloud-based systems. The presented model consisted of data acquisition for purifying and extracting the necessary information for executing out the forensic analysis. In forensic analysis model, five phases were involved namely, log acquisition and integration, log preprocessing, log correlation, log sequencing, analysis and reporting. These phases helped in detecting the evidence against threats more effectively. Although the integrity was improved, the confidentiality rate of data remains unconsidered.

Muhammad Imran et al. (2017) introduced data provenance to check the integrity level in cloud computing and provided protective measures to the cloud users. Data provenance was the local resource of cloud environment including the information called metadata. Metadata was utilized in explaining foundation and past history of the data product. Data provenance recorded all the integrity failures and the measures were taken to achieve high integrity. Data provenance avoided the use of third party services and offered the essential cloud computing requirements but minimized the filtering efficiency.

Nithya Chidambaram et al. (2016) introduced a secure storage system for offering security in cloud. In order to access the data from cloud, the clod user has to register with the cloud database. This helped in avoiding the illegal access of cloud data. In secure storage system, the files were encrypted with RSA algorithm. Then, digital fingerprint was provided through MD5 message digest before storage. The data continued inactive until the private key was provided. Both RSA and MD5 helped in avoiding third party to degrade the cloud storage system but failed to improve the data collection accuracy.

Yong Yu et al. (2016) described public integrity auditing scheme with multi-user data modification. The use of public integrity auditing scheme restricted third-party auditor (TPA) by combined with revoked user. Then, a virgin of deleted files was also kept. However, public integrity auditing scheme failed to address the issues of malicious attack.

Hui Tian et al. (2017) considered a public model for operation actions in cloud storage. In the public model, third party auditor (TPA) was established for checking the integrity to enhance the reliability of forensic outcome and the issues of forensic investigator were resolved. Then, block-based logging approach was employed for maintaining selective verification and security was offered through hash-chain-based structure. Merkle hash tree (MHT) was introduced to store the hash values of aggregated authentication block tags. The root of MHT was distributed to the public after the fixing of one block. Log-less verification was attained with privacy preservation. The public model helped in obtaining secure auditing for OBLs and the communication and computation cost was decreased. But the public model enhanced the investigation time.

Rameshwari Malik and Pramod Kumar (2015) introduced forensic virtual machine (FVM). FVM was employed for identifying the various security problems and differentiated by exploiting Bayesian classifier. Then, an intrusion detection system was planned that supervised the attacks against the network.

In FVM, the process of malicious attacks detection was categorized into three ways namely, detection of unauthorized access, malicious nodes and intrusion detection systems. Though FVM provided the security requirements, filter efficiency was not increased.

Cloud computing is simply vulnerable to security threats. Hamisu Alhaji Ali (2015) reviewed the cloud deployment model and the challenges involved in cloud computing for storing data and virtual applications were examined. Mostly, the causes of information and network in cloud computing appropriate to malicious attacks were mentioned. Then, security issues against real cloud computing was explained and protective measures against those issues was predicted. In addition to, with the help of risk analysis, cloud computing threats were investigated. The occurrence of threats and their affects was established. However, methods were not taken for enhancing the confidentiality rate of data.

Suleman Khan et al. (2016) analyzed the functionality of current network forensics methods (C-NFMS) in cloud computing. The merits, demerits, applicability, threats over cloud network were determined. Then by SWOT analysis, C-NFMs was classified and examined and estimated that C-NFM was appropriate on cloud network with improved applicability. But, filtering efficiency was not raised to the desired level.

Pranay Chauhan and Pratosh Bansal (2017) discussed the various security problems in cloud forensics. The evidence obtained in cloud computing is attained from multiple data center. Identification of evidence for forensic investigation became difficult. The security issues arrived because of the malicious activities was analyzed and examined. Then, secure integrated framework was established for resolving these security problems in cloud forensics. Eventhough security issues were considered, the investigation time was not addressed.

2.7. Fault Tolerance Techniques in Cloud Forensics

Fault tolerance in cloud computing helps in restricting the occurrence of errors. Jasbir Kaur and Supriya Kinger (2014) considered an efficient algorithm for fault tolerance based on cloud computing environment. Efficient algorithm using fault tolerance scheme, FCFS and SJF was considered including MPIL technique. Then during failure, servers were offered with reactive fault tolerance and load was reduced by the replacement of defective server task to a new server. The solutions for collaborative fault tolerance were employed in an autonomic cloud infrastructure. But the algorithm failed to enhance the confidentiality rate of data.

Cloud computing and cyber-physical system is used for real world maintenance in virtual environment. Hyun-Woo Kim et al. (2017) discussed an adaptive resource management (ARM). CPS consists of sensor, actuators and controller for interacting with physical elements.

The information in CPS gets degraded due to its sensor failure at sensing target area. ARM overcomes these limitations of sensor. In ARM, the information loss due to unbalanced resource lifespan and the problem caused by malicious threats was solved faster. Then, many-core of GPU was employed for avoiding the faults with higher speed. A substitute node of fault node was chosen to parallelize the sensor information. However, ARM decreased the data collection accuracy.

2.8. Cloud Forensics in Various Applications

Niken Dwi Wahyu Cahyani et al. (2017) explained the significance of mobile forensics in the investigation of terrorist activities. The forensic techniques utilized for reducing the malicious artefacts from client devices through Android and windows devices was exhibited. Information propagation, information concealment and communications were three simulation circumstances involved in the forensic techniques of terrorist activities. These simulations employed three famous cloud apps, five communication apps and two email apps. In the forensic technique of terrorist activities, mobile forensic was employed for gathering and examining the evidential data with the aid of network packet analyzer tools. The prohibited use of mobile devices was recognized through the association of evidence. Then, the obtained evidences between Android and Windows devices were mentioned which helped in acquiring a better evidentiary value but the filtering efficiency was not enhanced.

The process of detecting crime activities in forensic investigation is a challenging task. Ming Sang Chang (2016) analyzed the data customers on Windows 10 computer. The cloud actions of Amazon cloud drive were investigated through keyword searches and the evidences against malicious activities were acquired. Then, data remnants were estimated on local machines. The forensic investigator was satisfied. Subsequently, the remnants were originated from local folders. Recovery of removed files was also obtained through username, the cache files, and log activity. In addition to, data remnants on client devices were estimated and the efficiency of digital forensic investigation was increased. However, methods were not taken for reducing investigation time.

Frank M. Gotz (2015) introduced a cloud based service called Genolab. Genolab was employed for determining the statistical methods to link forensic analysis with DNA mixture interpretation. Genolab was extensively developed for processing the forensic investigation with cloud technology. During pilot phase in Genolab, the functionality was progressed for examining mixed samples. The functionality also included random man and likelihood evaluation through semi-or fully continuous models.

Then the resulting was based on ISFE guidelines and both subpopulation corrections with drop-out/drop-in events were involved. But, Genolab failed in addressing the malicious issues.

In business, cloud storage is tremendously utilized because of its specific features. The users were enabled to exchange the data from multiple computers with the aid of separate application installed in the computer through cloud-based storage called Amazon Cloud Drive. Jason S.Hale (2013) discussed the digital artifacts occurred when Amazon Cloud derive was utilized. In this assessment, the methods employed for estimating the files exchanges from or to Amazon Cloud drive on computer were considered. Then the relevant information was recovered by Amazon Cloud Drive artifacts through two Perl scripts. Though digital artifacts were considered, the confidentiality rate of data remains unaddressed.

Zhengwei Qi et al. (2017) introduced ForenVisor for consistent live forensics. ForenVisor was a special purpose hypervisor. The consistency of live forensics was enhanced in three steps. The first was construction of lightweight architecture for minimizing trusted computing base (TCB) size and then gathering of evidence from hardware directly. Filesafe module was utilized in safeguarding the evidence and other sensitive files but the investigation time was increased.

Sandra Zancajo-Blazquez et al. (2015) described a methodology for fast and efficient data acquisition in forensic science. In this described methodology, the point clouds were segmented with mobile indoor mapping technique. Then, the segmented point clouds were differentiated into 3-D models in CAD format with respect to parameterized geometric components. In forensic sciences, data necessitated was collected in a sufficient digital format with reduced time for data acquisition and processing. However, the filtering efficiency was minimized.

Dr Mark Taylor et al. (2014) discussed the acquisition of digital evidence from social media for computer forensics process and observed the legal issues occurred during data collection. Many organizations have started to use networking applications for forensic investigation. Such investigations results in failure due to the problems of digital evidence integrity in social networking applications. The malicious attacks and issues of forensic investigation in social networking applications were reviewed and measures were taken against those attacks. Eventhough security requirements were provided, the investigation accuracy was low.

Quang Do et al. (2015) described Cloud-Focused Mobile Forensics Methodology. The cloud-focused mobile forensic methodology was used for gathering evidential data located on devices. Smartphones are increasingly progressing due to its social applications.

Criminal action on the devices also increases. The application of cloud-based storage was needed to acquire the evidences related to illegal attacks. Cloud-Focused Mobile forensic methodology helped in acquiring information directly from devices for forensic investigation but failed in increasing the data collection accuracy.

Vassil Roussev and Shane McCulley (2016) investigate cloud-native digital artifacts-data objects for controlling the web/SaaS applications in a constant state. The web applications downloaded the required fly state and in local storage, no traces were produced. This analysis also confirmed that the digital artifacts had diverse structures but mostly in complete log form of user editing actions. The conventional approaches avoided the critical information on the development of document over time. Cloud-native artifacts did not follow a consistent external representation which affected long-term conservation and explanation. Eventhough, the artifacts were reduced, the filtering efficient in investigation process not increased. Plough

2.9. Research GAP

Secure-Logging-as-service (SecLaas) was established for conservation of different logs. In SecLaas, the logs generated from cloud were stored for virtual machines and offered with both integrity and confidentiality. Only the investigators were allowed to obtain these log files through RESTful APIs. This inturn increased the confidentiality of logs. The integrity of logs was also guaranteed through hash-chain scheme and the cloud providers issued the evidence of previous logs at times. Proof of Past Log (PPL) was introduced to avoid the investigators from altering the logs. Then in SecLaas, an accumulator scheme called Bloom-Tree was utilized. Bloom-Tree reduced the time and space requirements. SecLaaS served as a solution for providing forensic logs in a more secure way and was practicable to incorporate with cloud infrastructure. However, the cloud forensic investigation time was not minimized.

Forensic Acquisition and Analysis System (FAAS) was introduced for avoiding the involvement of cloud service provider (CSP) in forensic acquisition process. The process of forensic acquisition was carried with the help of agent-based approach at each VM. Then, the essential information was send to central cloud FAAS. All the cloud-management data was saved through agent-based acquisition and physical storage for VM data avoided the accessibility of CSP. Every file was made to be fully accessible by recreation of VM hard drive and the limitation of partial file inaccessibility was solved. Data carving and destruction was also eliminated. FAAS offered more admissible evidences to the investigators than CSP with the contribution or necessity of CSP. But, FAAS cannot find the log files of a real suspect during ensuring the user privacy.

Forensic Open-Stack Tools (FROST) was developed for providing a secure forensic acquisition. FROST was a group of forensic tools incorporated with cloud architecture. Through FROST, the cloud consumers, law enforcement and forensic investigators were allowed to obtain reliable forensic data without the involvement of cloud service provider (CSP). FROST included three components. First one, the cloud user was enabled to access an image of virtual disks and verified the integrity of that image with cryptographic checksums. Secondly, the logs of all API request were accessed by the cloud user and verified the integrity of these logs. Then, the cloud users were also enabled to recover the OpenStack firewall logs. FROST was also used in real-time monitoring auditing. FROST offered all the security concerns and enhanced forensic investigation for cloud computing. However, FROST executed only a data acquisition phase and other phases of the process affected by cloud computing were unaddressed.

Security as a Service model was introduced to offer security necessities for multiple customers. Security as service model safeguarded cloud infrastructure and the tenants were granted with flexibility to gain extra security functionalities. In Service model, malicious tenants were detected through the baseline security required by the provider. This helped in avoiding the malicious software. Every tenant must have the security functionalities to fight in opposition to malicious attacks. Conversely, there were special tenants that required extra security services from cloud provider to defend themselves from other malicious tenants. Security as a service model was suitable for offering extra security functionalities to those special tenants. The provided extra functionalities necessitated the tenants to expose more information about its application and works which resulted in privacy issues of the tenant. The service model approach find out both the privacy and security problems created in cloud provider. But, the cloud infrastructures frequently suffered from a number of security and compliance issues.

Secure provenance scheme was developed for ensuring confidentiality to the sensitive data in cloud. Secure provenance scheme was based on group signature and attribute-based signature technique (ABS) and provided anonymous authentication with fine-grained access on document control. Then, anonymous key-issuing protocol was used for preserving privacy of users which receiving the user's attribute private key from multiple attribute authorities. The computation and communication overhead of data owner was minimized in two ways. One was through broadcast encryption employed for controlling the user's access and the other one was attribute-based signature. Attribute-based signature was a component of access request and calculated by users.

In addition to, cryptographic operation of exponentiation in a bilinear group was utilized in decreasing the computational overhead in two ways. The first one was two-server model which calculated the exponentiation considerately and the second one was proxy re-signature method. Secure provenance scheme reduced the complexity at data owner side in terms of modular multiplications. However, an efficient investigation was not performed to reduce the cloud owner's computation overhead.

2.10. Research Contributions

Initially, Spatio-temporal Forensic Data Collector and Logging Filter (STFDC-LF) technique is introduced in cloud environment for detecting the evidence of malicious user by using forensic logging filter. Through STFDC-LF technique, a privacy preserved cloud forensic logging framework is presented. In STFDC-LF technique, Spatio-temporal Forensic Data Collector Scheme is employed for obtaining the data from various resources. This increases the investigation accuracy. Then, the internal clock and external clock is used through the application of Event Activity Time Synchronization to supervise multiple cloud files at a specific time. The investigation time in cloud forensic is minimized. At last, the evidence of malicious user in the cloud infrastructure is established by forensic logging filter. STFDC-LF technique enhances the investigation accuracy and filtering efficiency with minimum investigation time. Secondly, Gene Optimized Multi-objective Proof Accumulator (GOMOPA) technique is developed for finding the suitable evidence and malicious user in the cloud. In GOMOPA technique, the evidence of malicious behaviors and multiple objective functions are stated to the proof accumulator.

By gene based approach, the objective functions in the accumulator are optimized. GOMOPA technique optimizes only the global optimum solutions by fitness estimation that helps in detecting the malicious user. Then, the evidence of malicious behavior is identified through optimization operators namely, selection, crossover and mutation. GOMOPA technique increases the confidentiality of cloud users' log files and investigation accuracy with minimum processing time.Finally, Spatiotemporal Forensic Data Collector and Swarm Optimized Multi-objective Proof Accumulator (SFDC-SOMOPA) is developed for the identification of malicious behavior in cloud infrastructure. SFDC-SOMOPA includes three processes namely, acquirement of cloud log files from various sources, log data isolation and statement of admissible evidence. In SFDC-SOMOPA, spatiotemporal forensic data collector is employed for acquiring cloud log files from cloud resources. System reliability is increased by fault tolerance time synchronization for offering a significant function with given time interval.

Then, the log files of different cloud users are isolated through Watershed forensic logging filter (WFLF) for guaranteeing the privacy of malicious users and other cloud users. The malicious behavior evidence and multi-objective functions are stated to the proof accumulator. Particle swarm optimization (PSO) optimizes these objective functions. At last, best evidence was obtained for detecting the malicious user by fitness calculation. GOMPOA technique enhanced the investigation accuracy and filtering efficiency with minimum processing time.

CHAPTER III

SPATIO-TEMPORAL BASED FORENSIC DATA COLLECTION AND ISOLATION IN CLOUD

3.1. Introduction

Cloud computing services are spread across various distributed computing services such as storage, networking, servers, software, database and analytics with different deployment models. The cloud computing is widely used for business and end users due to the some features such as self service provisioning, elasticity, pay per use and migration flexibility. Due to increasing huge demands for cloud, attacks by malicious users also increased drastically in recent years.

So securing secured cloud environment is becoming a great challenge day by day Therefore, the cloud forensic investigation is termed as digital forensic procedure introduced in cloud computing. The cloud forensic investigation is a necessary process to deal with post-attack investigation on cloud environment. Through the cloud forensic investigator, the cloud log files of multiple cloud users are collected and examined in order to recognize the evidences of malicious user.

Many research works are examined to ensure secured cloud services on cloud environment. An existing Forensic Acquisition and Analysis System (FAAS) was developed with agent-based approach in Infrastructure as a Service model to manage the forensic acquisition process by the cloud user without the participation of the Cloud Service Provider (CSP). However, the log file of a real suspect was not easily attained by FAAS while providing the user privacy. Besides, Secure-Logging-as-a-Service (SecLaaS) scheme was introduced to ensure confidentiality and integrity for generated logs on cloud. But, the consumption of time was not reduced for performing the cloud forensic investigation to detect the malicious users on cloud system.

Therefore, the Spatio-Temporal Forensic Data Collector and Logging Filter (STFDC-LF) technique is developed in cloud infrastructure to address the above mentioned issues by accumulating and separating the evidence of malicious activities with the aid of activity logs. Through the STFDC-LF technique, cloud log files are recovered from the particular Virtual Machine (VM) resource to discover the malicious activity of users who causes for the particular crime incident on cloud.

At first, the Spatio-Temporal Forensic Data Collector scheme is deployed to collect various log files from the diverse of cloud resources such as application logs, storage logs, computing logs and network logs while using the information relevant with physical location and temporal information. From that, the investigation accuracy gets improved while searching the evidence of malicious users. Followed by Event Activity Time Synchronization method is deployed to manage the multiple cloud files at a specific time on cloud by using the internal clock and external clock thereby the investigation time is reduced. Secondly, the Forensic Logging Filter (FLF) is applied on collected cloud log files to separate the log files of the multiple cloud users which are unrelated to the crime event which ensures the privacy preservation with improved filtering efficiency. As a result, the evidential artifacts of the malicious activities are identified by using proposed STFDC-LF technique with Spatio-Temporal Forensic Data Collector scheme, FLF, Event Activity Time Synchronization method and in cloud environment.

3.2. Forensic Acquisition and Analysis System (FAAS)

Saad Alqahtany et al., (2016) introduced new approach as Forensic Acquisition and Analysis System (FAAS) with two contributing factors such as agent coordinator and cloud FAAS to analysis and acquire the forensic data from cloud server. The existing work performed the forensic acquisition process by implementing the agent based approach in each VM to the cloud user without the participation of the cloud service provider.

Later the required information was transmitted to the Cloud FAAS. All cloud management data (e.g. VM start time, stop time) was recorded with the help of agent-based acquisition. Agent-based acquisition was removing the physical storage locations for the VM data which was accessed only by CSP. After that, the image of VM hard drive was recreated at any point in time. Then, the agent-based acquisition provides easy admittance to the every file. This in turns, the restriction was provided to access the partially overwritten files and issues involved with data carving and fragmentation being eliminated. Therefore, the forensic investigation ensures the better performance of data acquisition.

The agent coordinator in a cloud controls the agents such as non-volatile memory agent, volatile memory agent, network traffic agent and activity log agent which were installed within an individual VM system. Besides, the cloud FAAS was considered as the central processing point for managing the forensic data on cloud environment. The communication between two contributing factors was carried out by communication engine.

Through the agent based approach, the communication of contributing factors was secured. This in turns, the confidentiality and integrity to the forensic data were achieved.

The image data was forensically hashed to files by agent coordinator and agent manager at all levels in order to provide the security control throughout the acquisition. In the forensic image storage, the data was stored after hashing the images to files. The forensic manager was the fully responsible for controlling the entire system and to provide the interface to the forensic investigator. In addition, the ability of investigator for selecting the system and time frame were examined by forensic manager. After reconstruction of images by using image reconstruction module, the data was given to perform the forensic examination and analysis. However, the log files of a real suspect were difficult to attain while assuring the user privacy.

3.3. Secure-Logging-AS-A-Service (SECLAAS) Scheme

Shams Zawoad et al., (2016) develops the Secure-Logging-as-a-Service (SecLaaS) scheme with the aim of achieving better results in confidentiality and integrity entities by protecting the different logs produced for examining the activity of virtual machines running in cloud environment. The SecLaaS scheme was performed with Proof of Past Log (PPL) which is referred as a tamper evident scheme for protecting the cloud service providers or investigators from the modification of logs after the fact.

In addition, the variation of the Bloom filter scheme was carried out to ensure better improvement on providing the security to the cloud data than the other traditional Bloom filter approach. Through the SecLaaS scheme, the cloud logs were stored in a secured manner by guaranteeing the APIs to forensics investigators and observing the integrity of logs.

During the forensic investigation, the SecLaaS scheme was implemented to acknowledge the cloud users' logs whereas the confidentiality of users' logs from malicious users and external attackers was provided. Through the SecLaaS scheme, the following attacks were addressed to store the cloud log files within a secured manner by the cloud forensic investigation.

- Cryptographic keys of cloud log files were identified by computing the cache usage.
- User password was tracked by examining keystroke timing of cloud user.
- Denial of service attacks were launched on the shared resources.

Initially, different types of logs from the Node Controller (NC) were discovered for each running VM over a cloud environment. Later it was discovered log files were stored into the persistent log database.

Therefore, the useful logs files were tracked if the VM was terminated while performing the investigation. The SecLaaS scheme provides the integrity and confidentiality of the logs by storing the logs into the log database. Followed by, the proof of that logs access in the proof database was conserved by SecLaaS scheme.

Through the SecLaaS scheme, Application Programming Interface (API) was ensued by the investigator in order to obtain the necessary logs of a particular IP. By providing the proofs of past logs along with the logs, the logs as admissible evidence were ensured thereby the secured service was enabled on the cloud environment. However, the time taken to perform cloud forensic investigation was too high.

3.4. Multi-Tenants Forensic Data Collection And Isolation Using STFDC-LF Technique

The cloud forensic is a digital forensic procedure which performs the processes such as collection, examination, analysis and reporting as well as the privacy level of information and integrity also protected in the cloud environment. Due to the some features such as legal feature, technical and organizational suggestion, the cloud forensic is used in investigation process to detect the malicious users for the particular crime incident on cloud. The legal feature takes responsibility in cloud forensic investigation which leads to observe the forensic activities.

The accurate forensic toolkit is provided by the technical feature in order to perform the forensic investigation on cloud platform. Through the organizational suggestion, the internal structure of the institute and the external supporter are illustrated for the specific incident on cloud. Consequently, Spatio-temporal Forensic Data Collector and Logging Filter (STFDC-LF) technique is proposed with the aim of identifying the evidence of malicious activities by combining models such as collection of cloud log files and multi-tenants log data isolation with privacy preservation.

The below figure 3.1 describes the cloud forensic framework for privacy preserved logging scheme. As shown in figure 3.1, the cloud forensic investigation is performed by considering the VM snapshots as digital evidence to identify malicious user's causes for crime event. Initially, the cloud owner outsources their data to the cloud server on cloud environment. After that, the cloud users send the request to the CSP when they want to access the multiple data on cloud. The CSP provides VMs for rent to the cloud users whether the user either malicious or trustful. Here, the data transaction is investigated by cloud forensic for detecting the malicious activities.

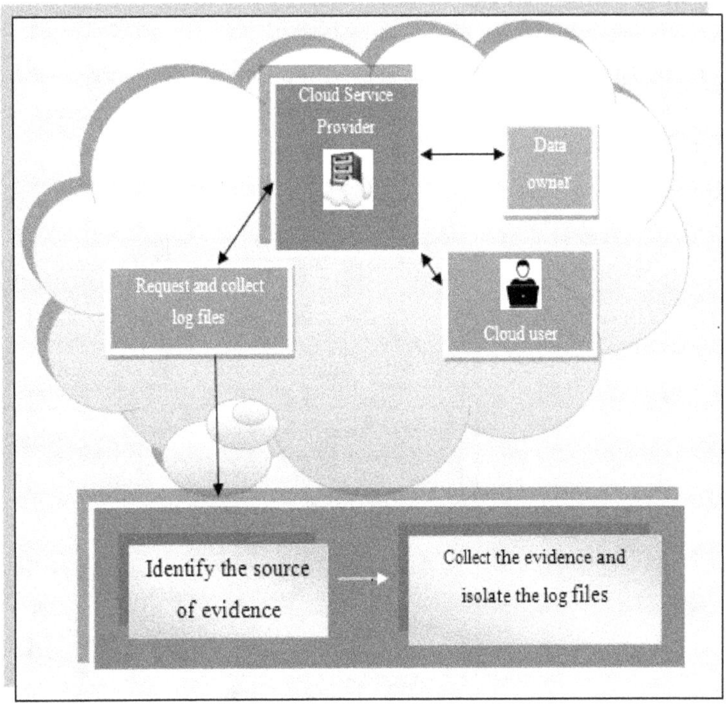

Figure 3.1: Overview of Logging Scheme With Privacy Preservation On Cloud Forensic Framework

Therefore, the proposed STFDC-LF technique implements the cloud forensic with the aim of providing privacy preserved cloud forensic to discover the proof of the malicious users. Later, multiple activity log files are utilized by the proposed STFDC-LF technique to collect the some sources of proof from different resources. The following block diagram as shown as figure 3.2 briefly describes the process of proposed STFDC-LF technique.

As illustrated in figure 3.2, data collection and Multi tenant log data isolation are performed with the help of proposed STFDC-LF technique. By executing the investigation process in proposed STFDC-LF technique, the cloud log files are collected and isolated from the log files of the multiple cloud users which are irrelevant with crime incident. At first, the various malicious activities of cloud log files are acquired from various resources by performing the data collection with the application of Spatio-temporal Forensic Data Collector scheme.

The Event Activity Time Synchronization method also involved in the process of data collection to identify exact time of crime event. Secondly, the Forensic Logging Filter (FLF) is used for separating the multiple cloud user log files from collected evidence of log files. Thereby the data privacy of the malicious users and other cloud users is preserved on cloud. The brief description of the proposed method is explained in following sections.

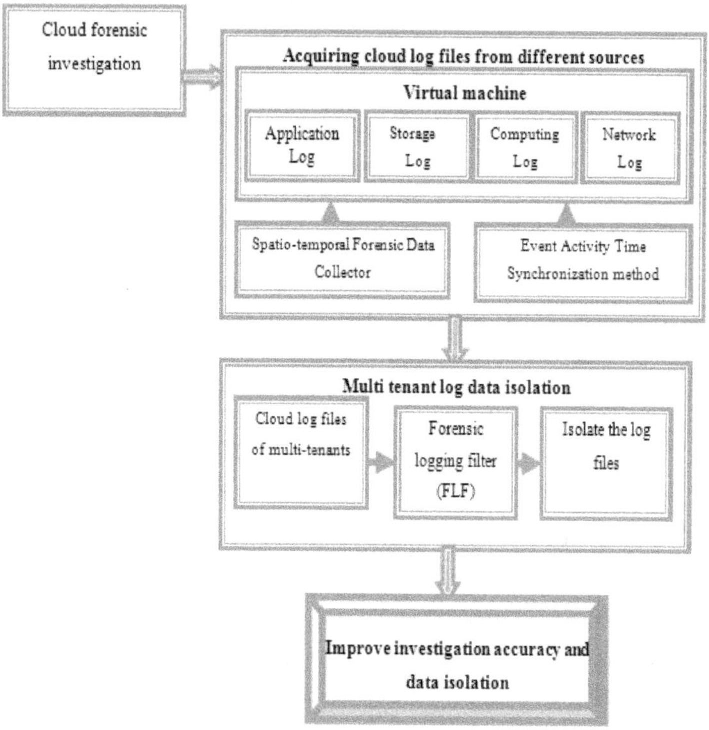

Figure 3.2: Architectural Diagram of the Proposed STFDC-LF Technique in Cloud Forensic Framework

3.4.1. Collection of Cloud Log Files From Different Sources

In the proposed STFDC-LF technique, the collection of cloud log files from various resources such as such as application logs, storage logs, computing logs and network logs is the first process to detect the evidence of malicious activities for the particular crime event. An application log is referred as a file of events which are recorded through the software application. The storage log is referred as a Log-in to the online storage account.

In cloud environment, log in and computing the tasks are performed with a cloud application. Then, the network logs are created by routers, network protocols and firewalls which comprise the information about the network or internet behavior of a particular device or network.

The proposed STFDC-LF technique carry outs data collection process which uses information related to the physical location and the temporal information of the crime event. The proposed STFDC-LF technique uses the Spatio-temporal Forensic Data Collector scheme and Event Activity Time Synchronization method for recovering the cloud log files with accurate time from specific VM resource. The collected cloud log files are reliable proof to the malicious activities.

3.4.1.1. *Spatio- Temporal Data Collector*

The data collection is performed by the implementation of Spatio-Temporal Forensic Data Collector scheme in the proposed STFDC-LF technique. The spatial data is referred as the data or information to sense the location of crime event and boundaries. Then, the temporal data is referred as the data to extract the exact time of crime event in particular location. In cloud environment, the cloud log files comprises information such as unique user ID, session ID, log file limit, time stamp, and event of the log which is used to discover the proof of malicious activity of users.

The proposed STFDC-LF technique uses Spatio-Temporal Forensic Data Collector scheme to detect the location and time of crime incident on cloud. The Spatio-Temporal Forensic Data Collector is performed as database to maintain the information about the location and time for the evidence of malicious users by utilizing the activity logs. Due to the complexity of cloud structure, the cloud forensic investigator faces big issues for accumulating the evidences from cloud server. Through the maintenance of privacy strategy by cloud provider, the accurate evidence of malicious activities is acquired from the cloud servers. By analyzing the spatial and temporal data in cloud environments, the artifacts are prevented to detect the malicious activities.

Through the spatiotemporal event collection approach, the abnormal activities of users are tracked by individually observing them. Then, the unusual activities are isolated from normal activities. The abnormal event patterns are acquired by correlating the events across both space and time in the STFDC-LF technique.

Let us assume, 'L' is referred as the location at which the spatiotemporal data is acquired on cloud. The 'L' is comprised with the number of regions which is formulated as given below.

$$L = \{r_1, r_2, r_3, \dots, r_n\} \qquad \text{....Eqn (3.1)}$$

From the above equation 3.1, the region is referred as '$\{r_1, r_2, r_3, \dots, r_n\}$'. Each region contains spatial objects is denoted as '$O_{1,} O_2, O_3 \dots O_n$' at time T. The time T has the consecutive time intervals '$\{t_1, t_{2,} t_3, \dots. t_n\}$'. Since, the accurate location and time is tracked which is related to the cloud log

In cloud environment, each cloud user examines the physical occurrence of data to accumulate the continuous data (n) samples over a time interval T which is described as given below.

$$CU_i = \{u_i^1, u_i^2, \dots u_i^n\} \qquad \text{....Eqn (3.2)}$$

From the above equation 3.2, 'CU_i' denotes the cloud user in a cloud environment and $\{u_i^1, u_i^2, \dots u_i^n\}$ denotes the continuous data (n) which is collected by the cloud user. At the cloud server, the new global weighted vector is used after the particular interval time, to restore the spatio-temporal data within a cyclic order. The following equation is described as given below to measure the corresponding data.

$$D_i = u_i W_o + V_i \qquad \text{....Eqn (3.3)}$$

From the equation 3.3, W_o is referred as the initial weighted vector of the cloud users (u_i) and V_i is referred the temporal and spatial uncorrelated data. The spatial and temporal relationship of data between cloud users and server is extracted with the help of Spatio-Temporal Data Collector. Therefore, the Spatio-Temporal Data collector collects the cloud log files without using any past information about the data statistics by extracting the internal variation of the cloud environments.

Two global statistical information (evident) is collected which is relevant to the crime incident. The following equation is formulated to compute two global statistical information.

$$R_{uu} = E[UU^T] = \begin{vmatrix} E[u_1 u_1] \dots\dots. E[u_1 u_m] \\ \vdots \\ E[u_m u_1] \dots\dots E[u_m u_{m1}] \end{vmatrix} \qquad \text{....Eqn (3.4)}$$

$$R_{Du} = E(DU) = \begin{bmatrix} E\ [Du_1] \\ E\ [Du_2] \\ \cdot\cdot \\ \cdot\cdot \\ E[Du_M] \end{bmatrix} \qquad \text{....Eqn (3.5)}$$

From the above equation 3.4 and 3.5, R_{uu} and R_{Du} refers two global statistical information. Since, the measured global weighted vector at the cloud server is computed as given below.

$$W_l^G = W_{l-1}^G + \mu \textstyle\sum_{i=1}^{m} (R_{Du,l} - R_{uu} W_{l-1}) \qquad \text{....Eqn (3.6)}$$

From the above equation 3.6, the global weighted vector is denoted by W_l^G and the positive step size parameter is denoted by μ. At each server in a cloud environment, the new updated vector is computed after the computation of global weighted vector. The new updated vector is calculated as given below.

$$W_{i,l}^N = W_{i,l} + \mu\left(u_i^T\left(D_i^N - u_i W_{i,l-1}\right)\right) \qquad \text{....Eqn (3.7)}$$

From the above equation 3.7, the new updated weight vector is indicated as $W_{i,l}^N$, the data with multiple users is indicated as D_i^N and the users login time is indicated as u_i^T. The cloud users are randomly employed over a network and the malicious users are traced in the physical cloud environment. Therefore, the proposed STFDC-LF technique is performed with Spatio-temporal Forensic Data Collector scheme to detect the proof of malicious users over a cloud environment.

According to the statistical behavior of observation, the Spatio-temporal Forensic Data Collector identifies whether the user is malicious or not. The statistical information of each user is ensured by computing the newly weighted vector for collecting the evidence of the crime incident.

The statistical value of the user is different from the normal users, when the user is malicious. The malicious user obtains incorrect data readings and transmits the incorrect data to the cloud server on the cloud environment. The Spatio-temporal Forensic Data Collector scheme is implemented to collect the inaccurate data and other correct data of cloud users by cloud server. From the collected data, the location and time for malicious activities are extracted in cloud environment.

3.4.1.2. Event Activity Time Synchronization Method

In the proposed STFDC-LF technique, Event Activity Time Synchronization method is carried out across the collected log files of a specific crime incident by cloud server. The simultaneous file handling operations are reliably carried out by performing the synchronization in cloud storage system. In the analysis of cloud logs files, the synchronization of time event taken as important factor which is considered as the source of evidence for the crime event. There is a necessity to discover the timestamp, if the crime event is occur on the cloud.

Every event over a network contains stamp (time field). The stamp is used to detect the specific time when the record was generated. The generated record contained with stamp, time field helps to extract the particular time.

In cloud computing, the time keeping state plays essential role to identify the evidence and preserve the privacy level while performing the cloud forensic investigation. The timing information of time stamps for each cloud user is the significant factor for exacting the digital evidence of malicious user.

3.4.1.2.1. Event Activity Time Synchronization with External And Internal Time Resources

The synchronization of physical machine is controlled by the cloud service providers. Then, the cloud service provider also utilized for clocks to comprise the accurate time while performing synchronization.

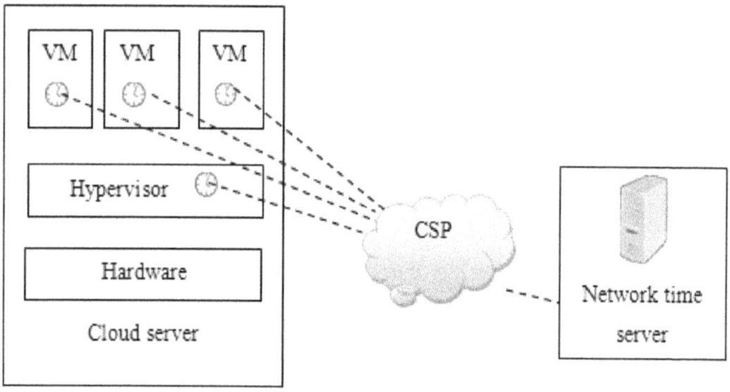

Figure 3.3: Event Activity Time Synchronization with External Source

The figure 3.3 illustrates the Event Activity Time Synchronization with external source. The Event Activity Time Synchronization with external source comprises of different clock synchronization and hypervisor. Each virtual machine is considered as a guest machine. The hypervisor running with several virtual machines in the system is known as host machine. From the figure, it is observed that the network time server provides the specific crime event of cloud log files by using the Network Time Protocol (NTP). The NTP is a networking protocol to ensure the time synchronization among different computer systems in the networks. In the public internet, NTP is used to prevent the time consumption within tens of milliseconds over a public internet and also one millisecond of accuracy attained in LANs through the NTP. There are three modes of operations involved in the NTP such as primary server, secondary server and client. In NTP, the primary server is properly synchronized with a reference clock. Then, the secondary server is contained with up and downstream servers and the clients synchronize the upstream server.

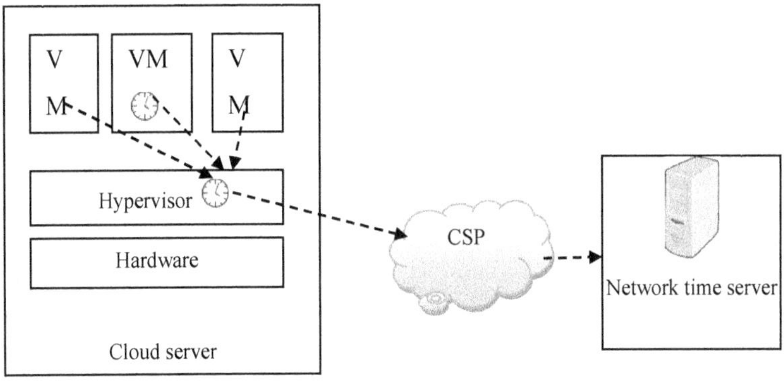

Figure 3.4: Event Activity Time Synchronization with Internal Source

The above figure 3.4 illustrates the Event Activity Time Synchronization with internal source. The wall clock is controlled by VM through the synchronization of physical machine's local clock with guest machine OS. The hypervisors is used to maintain the time without making time drifts. In generally, the clock of each VM is monitored and estimated with the hosting machine's local clock by the hypervisors.

The hypervisor modifies the guest OS clock without any warning if the variation is recognized. Otherwise, the hypervisor just reports the OS. If the VM was suspended, or a snapshot was re-established, the hypervisor carry outs the actions. From that, it is clearly observed that the STFDC solution is attained based on the cloud service provider. Consequently, the whole virtual resources in the cloud server are operated totally under the control of cloud service provider.

In the cloud environment, the VM's internal clock and any other virtual resources are maintained by the cloud service provider. The hypervisor is a significant resource to perform the cloud forensic investigation on cloud. The clock linked log-records is controlled by ensuring information such as the checking time of clock and which type of protocol was used. From that, the Event Activity Time Synchronization method is used to extracts the malicious event with minimum investigation time.

The Event Activity Time Synchronization method is employed while executing all operations for CSP and guest VM performing for clock synchronization. The collected log files from VM resources contain multiple cloud users of cloud log files. Therefore, the Forensic Logging Filter is used in the proposed STFDC-LF approach to separate the log files which is irrelevant to the crime incident.

3.4.2. *Multi Tenant Log Data Isolation*

According to the probabilistic structure, log files of multiple cloud users are separated by Forensic Logging Filter (FLF), whereas the data privacy of the malicious users and other cloud users also provided. The FLF verifies the unique user ID and specific event of the temporally retrieved log files to isolate the cloud log files from the collected log files.

Through the FLF, the cloud log file which is not related to the crime event is discovered based on the event thereby the confidentiality of the multiple users who share the same cloud infrastructure gets improved. Multi-tenant is the collection of number of log files to separate them whereas each user who is linked with his tenant is only allowed to access the data.

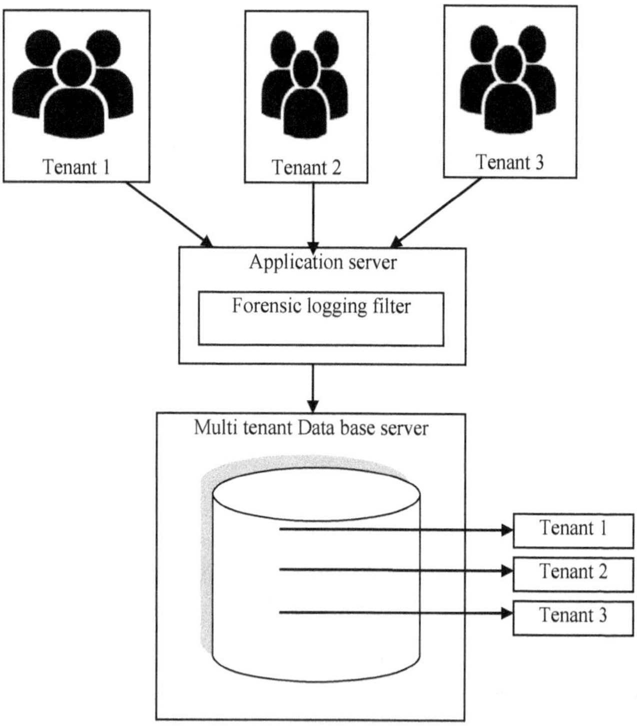

Figure 3.5: Multi Tenant Forensic Log Filter Process

The above figure 3.5 illustrates the process of multi tenant forensic log filter. From that figure 3.5, the multi tenant forensic log filter reconstructs the event and correlates the four various logs such as application logs, storage logs, computing logs, and network logs to the specific layer data format.

Thus, the assured log information is discovered and the time, protocol type, IP address, User ID, MAC address are rearranged with the help of logging filter. Each tenant data in cloud share the similar application and store in an independent database. The multi tenant log data isolation is an easy storage method with better results in data isolation. In addition, the multi tenant log data isolation is suitable method to backup and restore their data for user. In the digital forensic, the isolation process is carried out for preventing the evidences from the malicious users.

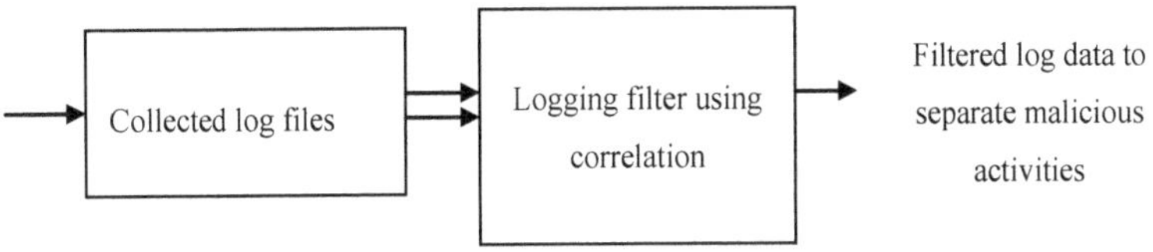

Figure 3.6: Forensic Log Filter Process

The above figure 3.6 describes the forensic log filter process which uses correlation measure. The sequences of events from different logs are generated by sending the collected data log files to the monitoring framework. According to the correlation with related preferences, the log files are isolated which is unrelated to the crime event. Hence, the malicious user and other cloud users on cloud environment are discovered by using the Pearson Correlation filtering approach. Then, the correlation between any two events of tenants is detected as given below.

$$r = cor\ (E_1, E_2) == \frac{\sum e_1 e_2 - \frac{(\sum e_1)(\sum e_2)}{n}}{\sqrt{\left(\sum e_1{}^2 - \frac{(\sum e_1)^2}{n}\right)(\sum e_2{}^2 - \frac{(\sum e_2)^2}{n})}} \quad \text{....Eqn (3.8)}$$

From the equation 3.8, the number of users $u_i = u_1, u_2, .. u_n$ is referred as n , two events of tenants are represented as e_1 and e_2 , refers the sum of cross product of e_1 and e_2 is referred as $\sum e_1 e_2$, the sum of tenant 1 activities is represented as $\sum e_1$, the sum of tenant 2 activities is represented as $\sum e_2$, the sum of squared of tenant 1 activities of e_1 is referred as $\sum e_1{}^2$ and the sum of squared of tenant 2 activities is referred as $\sum e_2{}^2$.

Form the equation 3.8, the correlation coefficient ensures the values from-1 to +1. The multi tenant malicious activities are ensured as negative correlation values (i.e -1 to 0) which are isolated from other cloud log files. Then, the multi tenant normal activities are ensured as positive correlation values from 0 to 1.

The log files are isolated which is related and unrelated to the event respectively based on the multiple tenant events in order to provide confidentiality of the multiple users. The isolation of cloud log files is done by concentrating the different user ID, and specific event of the temporally retrieved log files with help of correlation measure in the Forensic Logging Filter (FLF). The below algorithm describes the process Pearson Correlation analysis.

// **Forensic logging filter algorithm**
Input: Number of cloud users '$CU_i = u_1, u_2, .. u_n$', Pearson correlation coefficient 'r'
Output: Isolate malicious activities and normal activities
Step 1: **Begin**
Step 2: **For** each events of tenants
Step 3: Measure the Pearson correlation coefficient 'r' using (8)
Step 4: **If** ('r' value between -1.00 to 0)
Step 5: Isolate the log files related with malicious activities
Step 6: **else If** ('r' value between 0 to +1.00)
Step 7: Isolate the log files related to normal activities
Step 8: **End if**
Step 9: **End for**
Step 10: **End**

Algorithm 3.1: Forensic Logging Filter Algorithm

From the above algorithmic description, the forensic logging filter algorithm is carried out with Pearson Correlation with the aim of identifying the malicious activities related to the crime event. If the coefficient values lies from -1 to 0, then the log files of malicious users related to the crime event are isolated. If the coefficient values lies from 0 to 1, then the log files related to the normal activities are isolated. This in turns, the evidence of malicious user is kept securely with the proof information to the crime event. By using the FLF in the proposed STFDC-LF technique, the log files of multiple cloud users are separated by ensuring the exact evidence of crime event. In addition, the forensic data are prevented from unauthorized access attempts thereby data privacy of the malicious users and other cloud users also achieved with the help of FLF.

3.5. Experimental Evaluation of STFDC-LF Technique

An efficient proposed Spatio-temporal Forensic Data Collector and Logging Filter (STFDC-LF) technique is implemented by using java language with CloudSim network simulator. To execute the experiments, the Cloud Sim simulator is performed by using Amazon EC2 dataset which ensures various cloud services with available resources on the cloud environment. The cloud forensics data is collected and discovered with minimum time by implementing the CloudSim.

The performance of proposed Spatio-temporal Forensic Data Collector and Logging Filter (STFDC-LF) technique is compared with the existing methods such as Forensic Acquisition and Analysis System (FAAS) and Secure-Logging-as-a-Service (SecLaaS) Scheme to carry out the experiments.

The experimental evaluation of proposed STFDC-LF technique is conducted on the following factors such as given below.

- Investigation accuracy,
- Investigation time,
- Filtering efficiency,
- Isolation time.

3.6. Results Analysis of STFDC-LF Technique

In order to analysis the performance of the proposed Spatio-temporal Forensic Data Collector and Logging Filter (STFDC-LF) technique which is compared with the existing methods such as Forensic Acquisition and Analysis System (FAAS) by Saad Alqahtany et al., (2016) and Secure-Lo

gging-as-a-Service (SecLaaS) Scheme by Shams Zawoad et al., (2016).

3.6.1. Performance Analysis of Investigation Accuracy

The Investigation accuracy is referred as the ratio of the number of malicious users is correctly identified to the total number of cloud users in cloud environment. The mathematical formula for investigation accuracy is measured as follows.

$$Investigation\ accuracy = \frac{(No.of\ user - No.of\ malicous\ \ users\ )}{Totol\ \ no.of\ cloud\ \ users} * 100 \quad \text{....Eqn (3.9)}$$

The investigation accuracy is measured in terms of percentage (%). Higher value of investigation accuracy ensures better performance of the technique.

Table 3.1: Tabulation For Investigation Accuracy

Number of cloud users	Investigation accuracy (%)		
	FAAS	SecLaaS scheme	Proposed STFDC-LF
10	60.45	64.89	68.87
20	62.75	66.98	70.79
30	64.85	68.89	72.87
40	66.74	70.06	74.68
50	68.36	72.69	76.49
60	70.56	74.06	78.69
70	72.24	76.06	80.49
80	74.86	78.69	82.87
90	76.23	80.49	84.79
100	78.54	82.87	86.97

The table 3.1 shows the experimental results of the investigation accuracy with respect to the different number of cloud users. The number of cloud user is varied from the range of 10 to 100 which is taken as input to conduct the experiments. For the simulation purpose, the proposed STFDC-LF technique is compared with existing methods such as Forensic Acquisition and Analysis System (FAAS) by Saad Alqahtany et al., (2016) and Secure-Logging-as-a-Service (SecLaaS) Scheme by Shams Zawoad et al., (2016).

From the table, it is clear that, based on the number of cloud users, three methods increases the investigation accuracy respectively. But, comparatively the proposed STFDC-LF technique improves the investigation accuracy than the other existing methods. Based on the table value, the graph is plotted in below figure 3.7.

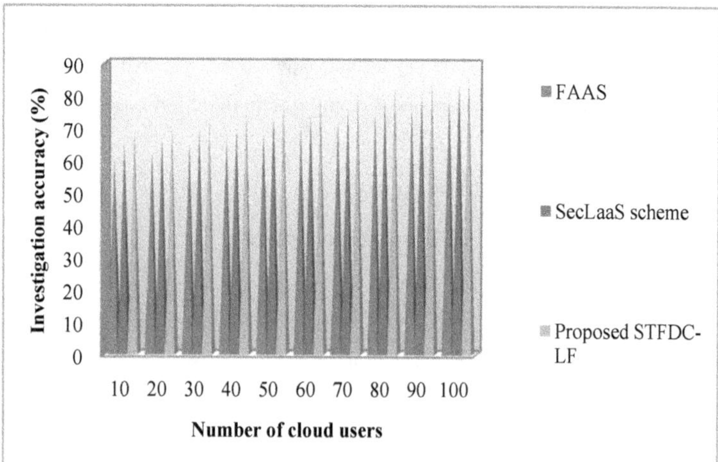

Figure 3.7: Measurement of investigation Accuracy

The figure 3.7 illustrates the measurement of investigation accuracy by using three methods such as proposed STFDC-LF technique, existing Forensic Acquisition and Analysis System (FAAS) and existing Secure-Logging-as-a-Service (SecLaaS) Scheme. The above figure clearly describes that the proposed STFDC-LF technique effectively enahnces the investigation accuracy than the other existing methods. This is because, the collection and isolation of evidence of malicious users from the multiple cloud users are performed by using the proposed STFDC-LF technique. Through the cloud forensic investigation, the Spatio-temporal Forensic Data Collector provides different cloud log files of multiple cloud users from various resources to identify the evidence of malicious users which leads to improve the investigation accuracy. As a result, the proposed STFDC-LF technique enhances the investigation accuracy up to 12% when compared to Forensic Acquisition and Analysis System (FAAS) by Saad Alqahtany et al., (2016) and 6% when compared to the Secure-Logging-as-a-Service (SecLaaS) Scheme by Shams Zawoad et al., (2016).

3.6.2. Performance Analysis of Investigation Time

The investigation time is measured as the amount of time consumed by the cloud forensic investigator to collect the evidences from the cloud users. The mathematical formula for investigation time is measured as.

$$IT = N * time\ (to\ collect\ evidence) \quad \text{....Eqn (3.10)}$$

The investigation time is measured in terms of milliseconds (ms). If the investigation time is less, then the technique said to be more efficient.

Table 3.2: Tabulation For Investigation Time

Number of cloud users	**Investigation time (ms)**		
	FAAS	**SecLaaS scheme**	**Proposed STFDC-LF**
10	30.7	26.1	16.8
20	32.1	28.2	18.9
30	34.4	30.1	20.5
40	36.8	32.2	22.5
50	38.6	34.6	24.9
60	40.3	36.1	26.6
70	42.2	38.9	28.6
80	44.4	40.1	30.5
90	46.6	42.2	32.5
100	48.1	44.3	34.2

The table 3.2 shows the experimental results of the investigation time with respect to the various number of cloud users. The number of cloud user is varied from the range of 10 to 100 which is taken as input to carry out the experiments.

For the simulation purpose, the proposed STFDC-LF technique is compared with existing methods such as Forensic Acquisition and Analysis System (FAAS) by Saad Alqahtany et al., (2016) and Secure-Logging-as-a-Service (SecLaaS) Scheme by Shams Zawoad et al., (2016).

From the table, it is clear that, based on the number of cloud users, three methods reduce the time to investigate the cloud log files respectively. But, comparatively the proposed STFDC-LF technique minimizes the investigation time than the other existing methods. Based on the table value, the graph is plotted in below figure 3.8.

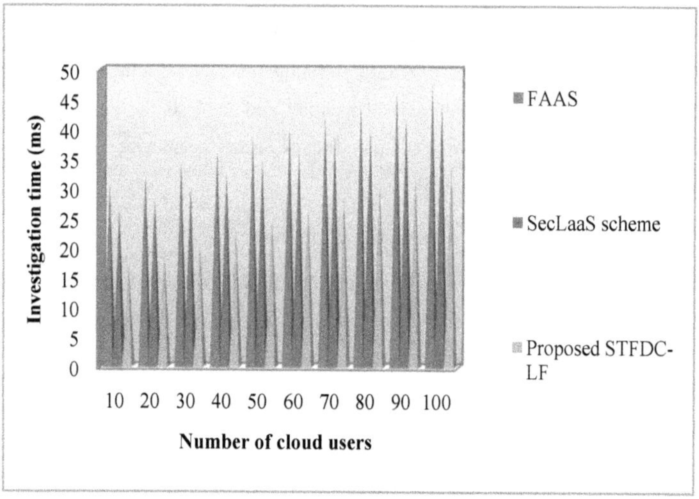

Figure 3.8: Measurement of Investigation Time

The figure 3.8 illustrates the measurement of investigation time by using three methods such as proposed STFDC-LF technique, existing Forensic Acquisition and Analysis System (FAAS) and existing Secure-Logging-as-a-Service (SecLaaS) Scheme. The above figure clearly describes that the proposed STFDC-LF technique is effectively reduces the investigation time than the other existing methods. This is because, the proposed STFDC-LF technique uses Event Activity Time Synchronization method with external source and internal source for different clock synchronization and hypervisors. Then, Event Activity Time Synchronization method executes the operation in terms of clock synchronization for multiple cloud users of log files with minimum investigation time. As a result, the proposed STFDC-LF technique minimizes the investigation time by 36% when compared to Forensic Acquisition and Analysis System (FAAS) by Saad Alqahtany et al., (2016) and 28% when compared to the Secure-Logging-as-a-Service (SecLaaS) Scheme by Shams Zawoad et al., (2016).

3.6.3. Performance Analysis of Filtering Efficiency

The filtering efficiency is measured as the ratio of the number of cloud log files is correctly isolated from collected cloud log file which is unrelated to crime activities to the total number of log files in virtual machines. The mathematical formula for filtering efficiency is described as given below.

$$FE = \frac{No.of\ isolated\ cloud\ \ log\ files}{Total\ no.of\ collected\ \ cloud\ log\ files} * 100 \qquad \text{....Eqn (3.11)}$$

The filtering efficiency is measured in terms of percentage (%). The higher value of filtering efficiency provides better performance of the technique.

Table 3.3: Tabulation For Filtering Efficiency

Number of cloud log files	Filtering efficiency (%)		
	FAAS	SecLaaS scheme	Proposed STFDC-LF
5	45.45	50.28	55.58
10	47.25	53.06	57.59
15	49.64	55.69	59.68
20	51.86	57.64	61.25
25	53.41	59.84	63.69
30	55.78	61.32	65.36
35	57.32	63.25	67.65
40	59.56	65.96	69.25
45	61.45	67.25	71.95
50	63.78	69.96	74.25

The table 3.3 shows the experimental results of the filtering efficiency with respect to the different number of cloud log files.

The number of log files is varied from the range of 5 to 50 which is taken as input to conduct the experiments. For the simulation purpose, the proposed STFDC-LF technique is compared with existing methods such as Forensic Acquisition and Analysis System (FAAS) by Saad Alqahtany et al., (2016) and Secure-Logging-as-a-Service (SecLaaS) Scheme by Shams Zawoad et al., (2016). From the table, it is clear that, based on the number of cloud log files, three methods significantly improves filtering efficiency to isolate the log files which is unrelated to the crime event on cloud. But, comparatively the proposed STFDC-LF technique enhances the filtering efficiency than the other existing methods. Based on the table value, the graph is plotted in below figure 3.9.

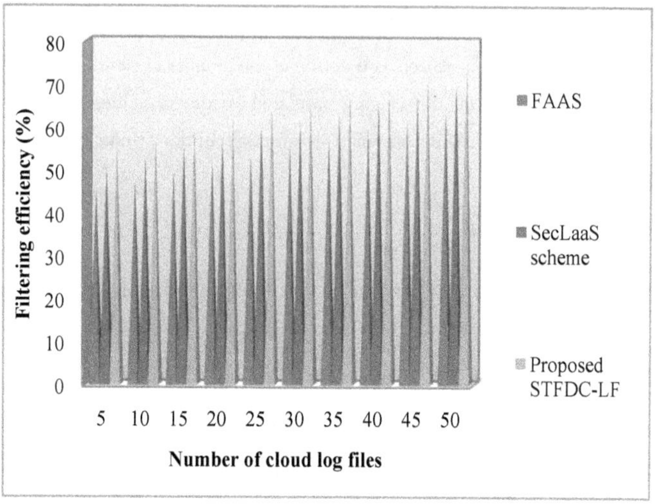

Figure 3.9: Measurement of Filtering Efficiency

The figure 3.9 illustrates the measurement of filtering efficiency by using three methods such as proposed STFDC-LF technique, existing Forensic Acquisition and Analysis System (FAAS) and existing Secure-Logging-as-a-Service (SecLaaS) Scheme. The above figure clearly describes that the proposed STFDC-LF technique is effectively improves the filtering efficiency than the other existing methods. This is because, the proposed STFDC-LF technique introduces Forensic Logging Filter for separating the evidence of malicious activities of cloud log files which are unrelated to the particular crime incident which enhances the filtering efficiency. As a result, the proposed STFDC-LF technique enhances the filtering efficiency up to 19% when compared to Forensic Acquisition and Analysis System (FAAS) by Saad Alqahtany et al., (2016) and 7% when compared to the Secure-Logging-as-a-Service (SecLaaS) Scheme by Shams Zawoad et al., (2016).

3.6.4. Performance Analysis of Isolation Speed

The isolation speed is defined as the rate at which the number of cloud log files gets separated from collected cloud log files which is unrelated to the crime incident. The isolation speed is evaluated as given below.

$$Isolation\ speed = \frac{Number\ of\ isolated\ cloud\ \log files}{Isolation\ time} \quad ....Eqn\ (3.12)$$

The isolation speed is measured in terms of Bytes per second (Bps). When the isolation speed is high, then the technique is said to be more efficient to detect the evidence of malicious users.

Table 3.4: Tabulation For Isolation Speed

Number of cloud log files	**Isolation speed (Bps)**		
	FAAS	**SecLaaS scheme**	**Proposed STFDC-LF**
5	6	8	10
10	9	11	13
15	12	14	16
20	15	17	19
25	18	20	22
30	21	23	25
35	24	26	28
40	27	29	31
45	29	31	34
50	31	34	37

The table 3.4 shows the experimental results of the isolation speed with respect to the different number of cloud log files.

The number of log files is varied from the range of 5 to 50 which is taken as input to conduct the experiments. For the simulation purpose, the proposed STFDC-LF technique is compared with existing methods such as Forensic Acquisition and Analysis System (FAAS) by Saad Alqahtany et al., (2016) and Secure-Logging-as-a-Service (SecLaaS) Scheme by Shams Zawoad et al., (2016).

From the table, it is clear that, three methods significantly reduces the isolation speed depends on the number of cloud log files. But, comparatively the proposed STFDC-LF technique minimizes the isolation speed than the other existing methods. Based on the table value, the graph is plotted in below figure 3.10.

The figure 3.10 illustrates the measurement of isolation speed while using three methods such as proposed STFDC-LF technique, existing Forensic Acquisition and Analysis System (FAAS) and existing Secure-Logging-as-a-Service (SecLaaS) Scheme. The below figure clearly describes that the proposed STFDC-LF technique effectively improves the investigation accuracy than the other existing methods.

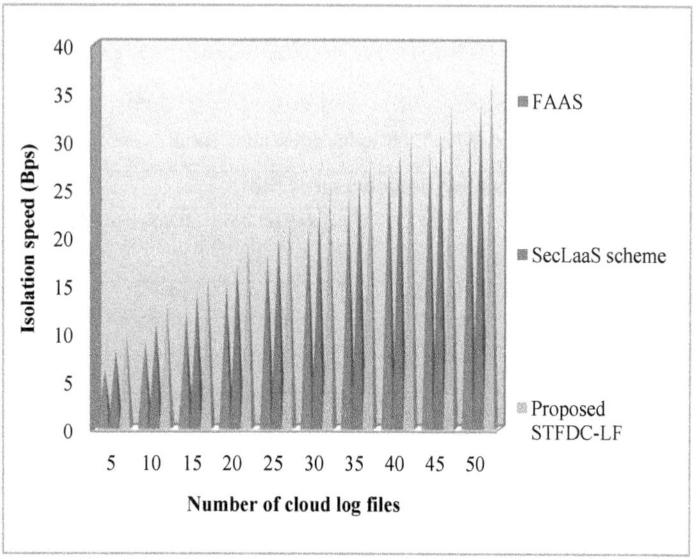

Figure 3.10: Measurement of Isolation Speed

This is because, the isolation of evidence of malicious users from the multiple cloud users which is not related to the crime event are performed by proposed STFDC-LF technique with the help of Forensic Logging Filter. Thereby the isolation speed gets improved while utilizing the location and time information. As a result, the proposed STFDC-LF technique enhances the investigation accuracy by 28% when compared to Forensic Acquisition and Analysis System (FAAS) by Saad Alqahtany et al., (2016) and 12% when compared to the Secure-Logging-as-a-Service (SecLaaS) Scheme by Shams Zawoad et al., (2016).

3.7. Summary

The proposed Spatio-temporal Forensic Data Collector and Logging Filter (STFDC-LF) technique is developed to discover the proof of malicious user by implementing the cloud forensic investigation. At first, the Spatio-temporal Forensic Data Collector acquires the cloud log files of multiple cloud users from various resources which lead to enhance the investigation accuracy. After that, Event Activity Time Synchronization manages the multiple cloud files at a specific time with the help of internal and external sources thus reduce the investigation time. Finally, the Forensic Logging Filter separates the evidence of malicious user which is irrelevant to the specific crime incident.

Moreover, the performance of proposed STFDC-LF technique is verified with the metrics such as investigation accuracy, investigation time, filtering efficiency and isolation speed by using Amazon EC2 dataset with cloudSim simulator. The experiments results show that the proposed STFDC-LF technique discovering the proof of malicious activities with improved investigation accuracy and filtering efficiency up to 9% and 13% by using the Spatio-temporal Forensic Data Collector scheme and Forensic Logging Filter. In addition, the Event Activity Time Synchronization method is used in the proposed STFDC-LF technique to reduce the time consumption by 32% for investigating the evidence of malicious user on cloud environment. Though the proposed STFDC-LF technique efficiently detects the evidence of malicious activities, it's not a sufficient method to detect the exact malicious users who initiates particular crime on cloud platform. In order to identify the malicious user in the cloud, the Gene Optimized Multi-objective Proof Accumulator (GOMOPA) technique is introduced by considering the multi-objective functions which is briefly described in the forthcoming chapter.

CHAPTER IV

MULTI-OBJECTIVE FUNCTIONS BASED GENE OPTIMIZATION FOR MALICIOUS USER DETECTION IN CLOUD FORENSIC SERVICES

4.1. Introduction

Cloud computing is the distribution model of computing services which enables various deployment and service models over an internet. In cloud computing, cloud forensic investigation is an effective way to trace the malicious user by performing processes such as acquisition, analysis, and reporting cloud log files about the incidents and illegal actions. During cloud service provisioning, the source of the malicious activities is identified by reporting the evidences of malicious user through the forensic investigator while persevering the privacy of information and confidentiality.

The existing Forensic Open-Stack Tools (FROST) was implemented to perform the data acquisition phase on cloud infrastructure. But, the issues correlated with other phases of the process remained unaddressed. In addition, Secure-Logging-as-a-Service (SecLaaS) scheme was developed to preserve the various logs generation for the actions of virtual machines running in clouds and to offer confidentiality and integrity of such logs. However, the investigation to discover the malicious user was not effectively executed by SecLaaS scheme. Then, the previous chapter illustrated on detecting the evidence of malicious activities on specific crime event with the application of Spatio-Temporal Forensic Data Collector and Logging filter (STFDC-LF) technique.

There is necessity to report the malicious evidence of cloud log files for tracing the malicious user from multiple cloud log files in cloud environment.

Therefore, the Gene Optimized Multi-objective Proof Accumulator (GOMOPA) technique is developed with the objective recognizing the malicious user by reporting the evidence and proving the crime activities inside the cloud. At first, the multi-objective functions such as evidence of the malicious activity, proof of integrity, provenance information, proof of data possession, time stamp information and location information are submitted to the multi-objective proof accumulator by the cloud forensic investigator.

Secondly, the gene nased approach is introduced to optimize the multi-objective functions. Through the proposed GOMOPA technique, Cloud Service Provider (CSP) validates the investigated proof with the real suspect to detect the accurate malicious user.

Finally, with the application of GOMOPA technique, the exact malicious user is discovered who initiates the malicious activities over the cloud infrastructure. Thereby the confidentiality of cloud log files gets improved while discovering the malicious user.

4.2. Forensic Open-Stack Tools (Frost) On OpenStack Cloud Platform

Josiah Dykstra and Alan T. Sherman (2013) developed Forensic Open-Stack Tools (FROST) for analyzing the design and implementation of management plane forensic toolkit in a secret instantiation of the Open-Stack cloud platform. The Open-Stack was developed into an Infrastructure-as-a-Service (IaaS) cloud platform. The Open-Stack cloud platform offers the reliable forensic acquisition in virtual disks, API logs, and guest firewall logs. The implementation of FROST addresses the issues related to maintenance of integrity of remote proof while saving the forensic data in hash trees and retrieving the evidence with cryptographic hashes. In the FROST, NIST definition of cloud computing as a model was utilized to provide on-demand access for pool of resources.

In cloud environment, FROST carries out the forensic investigation by utilizing the tools such as user-driven, permitting users, forensic examiners and law enforcement without the involvement of cloud provider. At first, the forensic data from host operating system level (outside the guest virtual machines) was collected by FROST to the cloud provider and assures that, whether the data was available at the management plane. Then, then it was presented by website. The Application Programming Interface (API) describes how the users control the cloud in the Open-Stack platform and describes when they start and stop virtual machines. Since, the cloud user did not communicate with virtual machine while collecting the forensic data; it was protected from the unreliable virtual machines.

OpenStack platform was integrated with FROST through the two components such as Nova and Horizon. OpenStack accepts the requests only from authenticated user. The username and password were necessary to Horizon web interface. Then, the command-line API needs either an access key and secret access key (which was retrieved by API), or an X.509 certificate and private key.

The private key was utilized to sign the API request. Then, the signature was send to the OpenStack with the certificate. Besides, Nova web interface contains root certificate to sign a documents. This root certificate was used to provide the integrity while storing the log data which called as Authenticated Logging Service (ALS) system. From ALS, these stored data was isolated to each user which is not accessed by other unauthorized users.

Therefore, FROST stores the forensic data with integrity checking information which offers the secure storage service. However, it is performed only in a data acquisition phase and other phases of the process affected by cloud computing were not addressed.

4.3. Improving Confidentiality On Cloud Data By Using Secure Logging-As-A-Service (SECLAAS) Scheme

During the forensic investigation, Shams Zawoad et al., (2016) developed Secure-Logging-as-a-Service (SecLaaS) scheme to provide confidentiality by protecting the cloud log files from malicious users. Then, Proof of Past Log (PPL) – a tamper evident scheme was implemented to protect the CSP or investigator from modification of logs. In addition, variation of Bloom filter scheme was presented to ensure the security than traditional Bloom filter approach.

Through the SecLaaS scheme, while investigating the malicious users on cloud environment the cloud log files were securely acquired from different sources, e.g., network, process, databases. The CSP securely stores cloud log files by using SecLaaS scheme which preserves the confidentiality. The integrity of the cloud log files were maintained by using Proof of Past Log (PPL) and the Log Chain (LC). While running VMs inside the Node Controller (NC), malicious activities of VM's from different logs were generated in the NC which is addressed by SecLaaS scheme.

At first, SecLaaS scheme was implemented in cloud to discover different logs from NC for each VM. After that, the extracted cloud logs were stored in a log database. It failed to ensure the log files, if the VM was terminated during the forensic investigation. Hence, the storing of log files by SecLaaS scheme in a log database ensures the integrity and confidentiality of the log files. In addition, SecLaaS scheme assures the proof of log entry in the proof database. The required log files of specific IP were obtained to the investigator by providing the API. The acceptable evidence was procured by providing the proofs of past logs along with the logs through the investigators. However, it not an effective scheme to identify the malicious users on cloud environment.

4.4. Reporting Acceptable Evidence of Suspect By Using Gene Optimized Multi-Objective Proof Accumulator

In the cloud environment, based on the pay-per-what-they-use different kinds of cloud services are offered by the CSP to the cloud users, Sometimes similar types of services are utilized often by some of the cloud users. There is a chance to trace confidential information of the cloud user by the malicious users.

Therefore, the cloud computing needs security for protecting the cloud data from the attacks of malicious activities. In addition, each cloud users of virtual machine (VM) required to be monitored in order to identify the malicious user over a cloud infrastructure.

Consequently, the cloud forensic investigation is performed on the cloud environment to collect and discover the evidence of malicious users. The forensic tools are used to analyze the evidences. Then, they are analyzed by court of law to prove the crime activities. Hence, Gene Optimized Multi-objective Proof Accumulator (GOMOPA) technique is introduced to estimate the malicious user for a particular event incident. The following figure 4.1 shows the architecture diagram of the GOMOPA technique.

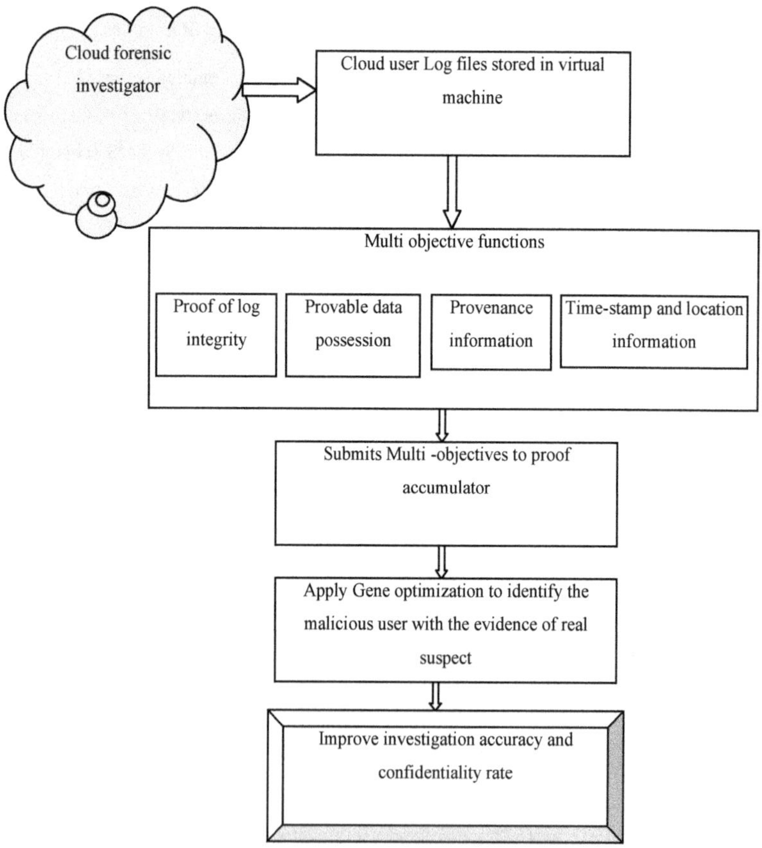

Figure 4.1: Architectural Diagram of The Gene Optimized Multi-Objective Proof Accumulator Technique

As shown in figure 4.1, the Gene Optimized Multi-objective Proof Accumulator (GOMOPA) technique is developed to detect the malicious user who launches the malicious activities for particular crime event on the cloud infrastructure. Through the proposed GOMOPA technique, the malicious evidence with real suspect is authenticated by CSP in order to trace the malicious user. From the evidence, the cloud log files which are stored in virtual machine are verified by the CSP thereby the malicious activity for the crime event is discovered. Initially, the multi-objective functions as evidence of malicious activities namely integrity, data possession, provenance information, time stamp information and location information are given to the multi-objective proof accumulator. Subsequently, the gene optimization approach is established after reporting the proof of malicious activities for the crime incident. The gene optimization approach selects the optimal solution (i.e. exact malicious user) from the evidences, thereby the accuracy to investigate the malicious user and confidentiality rate gets improved on cloud forensic environment. The process of GOMOPA technique is briefly explained in the following next sections.

4.4.1. Analysis of Multi Objective Function

At first, multi-objective functions of the evidences (i.e. cloud user log files) are submitted to multi-objective proof accumulator by cloud forensic investigator. The multi-objective functions contains evidence of malicious cloud users such as malicious user activities, evidence of integrity, provenance information, proof of data possession, time stamp and location information. The evidences (information) about the malicious user activities are preserved to provide secure access on cloud. Then, the data preservation controls the data integrity, thus it assures that the original data is not modified until the entire investigation process is completed.

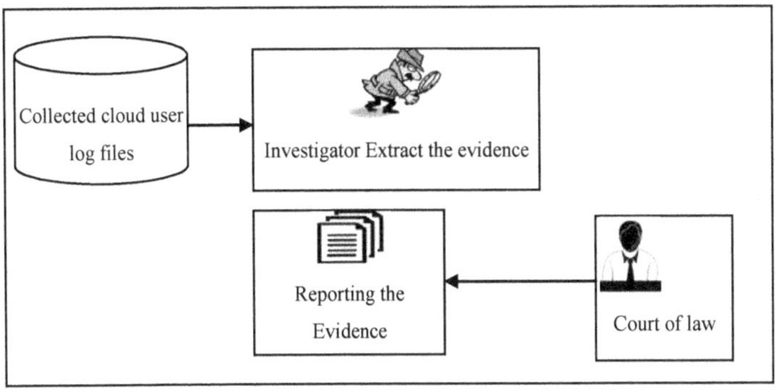

Figure 4.2: Cloud Forensic Models For Crime Investigation

The above figure 4.2 shows the cloud forensic model to detect the malicious user by performing the crime investigation. Initially, the investigator extracts the collected log files (i.e. evidence). Later the malicious users are discovered by extracting the information with real suspect. Thus the multi-objective functions such as proof of integrity, provenance information, proof of data possession, time stamp information and location information are analyzed while investigating the evidence of malicious users on cloud.

4.4.1.1. Proof of Integrity

The integrity of evidence is controlled by listing the part of event related information in the chain of custody register which comprise how, where and who initiates the malicious activity over the cloud environment. The whole history of evidence is maintained in the chain of custody. The chain of custody is formed in the past days while filling the document form or electronic form which contains name of investigators, a brief description of the evidence under inspection and a hash code. The chain of custody software is formed that is related with authenticity by generating and controlling the random metadata about fingerprint of evidences (what), events (how), digital signature (who), time stamping (when) and location (where). Thus it aids to the court by ensuing better understanding and for performing better forensic analysis on specific criminal case.

The cloud service provider detects the malicious activities and offers cloud services to authorized users over the cloud infrastructure. The efficacy of information is provided and protected from other malicious users as inspecting the physical evidences through the forensic investigation to find out the malicious user for the crime incident.

If the control of malicious evidences becomes inaccurate the value is destroyed. From that, the evidences are stored on the cloud in a appropriate manner to guarantee their integrity. Then, the proof of malicious activities needs to be accepted by the court proceedings. The integrity assures that original data are not changed into the evidence and submitted in front of law.

4.4.1.2. Provable Data Possession (PDP)

The Provable Data Possession (PDP) is comprised with evidence of data possession to ensure that the cloud investigator acquires the actual evidence or not. Then, the cloud investigator reports with the proof of malicious users to the multi-objective proof accumulator. The accumulator is a probabilistic data structure that contains information about the proof of past data possession in terms of a bit array to shows that the cloud user is normal or not.

Through the proposed GOMOPA technique, the information is stored in the tiger hash storage which is engaged as a proof accumulator. By utilizing the tiger hash storage, the cloud service provisioning is deployed in secured manner with better confidentiality rate. Thus compatibility is ensured by making the hash length of 128 and 160 bits through the Tiger/128 and Tiger/160. The confidentiality rate is assured to the system that the messages are received only by the authorized cloud user from the cloud server.

For a particular day, with one static IP, one tiger hash is capable to store the evidence of all the cloud user log files. The files are transmitted to the server by cloud user and then the new log files are created during the data possession generation. Then, the CSP provides the storage information of that particular cloud user after receiving an updated file. The log files are hashed by CSP and then the bit position from the hash value are created.

In addition, the tiger hash value is also updated with the current bit position. Then, the updated tiger hash value is stored by CSP in the storage space. The tiger hash entry of every cloud user (D_U) is retrieved by CSP at the end of the each day. Then, the tiger hash entry of every cloud user (D_U) is hashed with its private key. Hence, the proof of the data position (PDP) of that particular day is created as given below.

$$PDP =< H\ (D_U), Sign_{PK}\left(\mathrm{H}\ (D_U)\right), T > \quad \text{....Eqn (4.1)}$$

From the above equation 4.1, the hash entry of every cloud user is represented by $\mathrm{H}\ (D_U)$, the signature of $\mathrm{H}\ (D_U)$ with private key of the CSP is represented by $Sign_{PK}$ and the time of proof generation is represented by T. While detecting the malicious user, the proof of data possession time is increased and false positive probability is reduced with the increase of cloud log files. The CSP transmits the evidence of data possession with its public key on the web after generating the proof of data possession. Then, the information of entry of each cloud user is maintained by CSP with private key secret to itself.

4.4.1.3. Data Provenance Information

In the forensic analysis, data provenance information is significant aspect to provide the history of digital evidence. In order to perform the digital forensics investigation with trusted evidences, the secure data provenance method is introduced on the cloud environment. The data provenance method assures that evidence of cloud data is acknowledged by the court of law. Through the data provenance method, the integrity of records is preserved and also general data security properties are satisfied that leads to assurance of reliability.

The proposed GOMOPA technique stores the data provenance in the Provenance Store by the CSP. Therefore, essential evidences are stored by the proposed GOMOPA technique which is similar to data provenance.

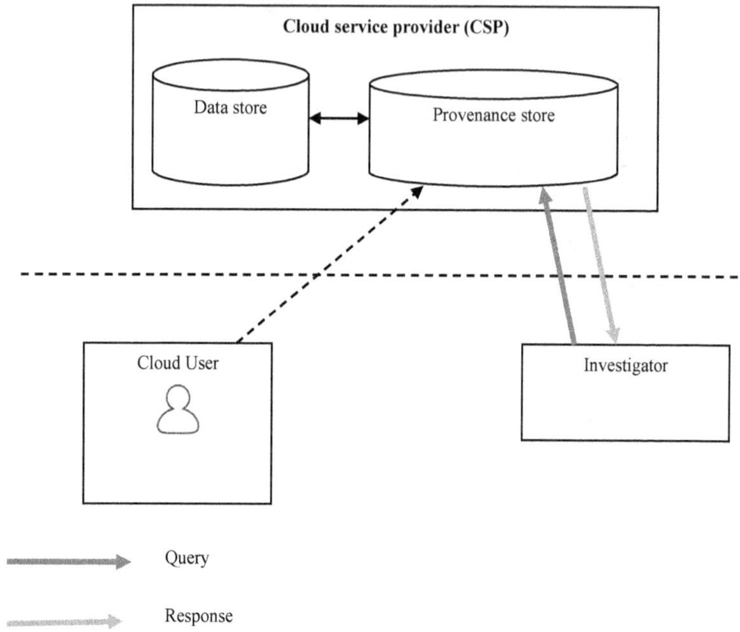

Figure 4.3: Data Provenance in Cloud

The figure 4.3 illustrates the storing and searching data provenance in cloud environment. The cloud user initiates the action on cloud and creates the data provenance in the trusted environment. The investigator takes responsibility to analysis the actions of the cloud users. Then, the data provenance up to origin is verified and the malicious activities on the source data are recognized by the forensic investigator.

In cloud infrastructure, the source data and its related data provenance are maintained by CSP. At first, the action is performed on the source data by the cloud user. Subsequently, the equivalent data provenance is forwarded to the Provenance Store. Then, the Query is transmitted to the Provenance Store by the forensic investigator. Finally, the result as Response is attained by the investigator. The table 4.1 shows the representation of the provenance information.

Table 4.1: Representation of Provenance Information

Review	Date	Time	User ID	Action	Prior Review	Hash	Signature
1					0	128 Bits	512 Bits
2					1		
..					..		

As shown in figure 4.1, version number is referred by the review. The Date and Time are represented when the event is occurred on cloud. The User ID represents the cloud user who performs the action on cloud infrastructure. The information of activities that happen on the source data is represented by the action column. Then, the action column is separated into four sections namely Name, Reason, Explanation and Location.

Name denotes what type of action is carried out on the source data. Reason illustrates why the action is carried out on data. Explanation ensures more details which contains the information as how the action is performed. Location shows where the action is performed. Prior review is represented as the version number of the action performed on the similar source data previously. After performing the action, the tiger hash function uses Hash to determine the transformation of current source data into a usually shorter fixed-length value. Thus it helps in discarding the forge ability. After signing the hash of other fields with the private key of the user, the Signature is ensured that guarantees the confidentiality and discards the repudiation.

4.4.1.4. Time Stamp Analysis

The timestamp holds the series of information when the crime event has happened on cloud environment. The timestamp is provided with the data, time of the day and small fraction of a second. The generation time of evidence is discovered while the CSP publishing the proof of data possession day by day.

The timestamp is the exact generation time of evidence or time range of the evidence occurred. Each record contains stamp, time field for reporting the evidence time. In cloud computing, the time keeping state evaluation is an essential for performing the cloud forensic investigation.

The secure time-stamp verification protocol is carried out between VMs. Timestamp has information with the event recorded by year, month, day of the week, day, hour, minute, second and milliseconds. These times are transformed into Universal Coordinated Time (UTC) which utilizes the local computer's time zone and daylight savings location. The location of the crime event is detected which in turn leads to the evidences that are extracted by forensic investigator and which are send to the court for trustworthiness verification.

Finally, the investigator submits the multi-objective functions such as proof of integrity, provenance information, proof of data possession, and the time stamp information to the proof accumulator. According to the collected evidence, these objective funciotns are optimized to detect the malicious user with real suspect by using gene based approach.

4.4.2. Gene based Approach

After the submission of multi-objective functions to the proof accumulator, the gene based approach is developed with the aim of identifying the optimal solutions with confidentiality at each generation by ensuring the population of multiple objective functions. The optimization is the process of generating the optimal evidence that assures the crime activities and detects the malicious user with real suspect.

Through the accurate fitness assignment approach, the optimal solution is discovered by using multi-objective optimization, a set of most feasible evidence is identified based on the multiple objective functions and constraints. The CSP validates the investigated evidence with the real suspect to determine the malicious user depends on the fitness value with the help of proposed GOMOPA technique.

The gene optimization has some parameters, operators and processes that provide an optimal solution to detect the malicious user who launches the crime inside the cloud. From that, optimization process plays significant role while determining the optimal result from the entire feasible solutions.

Then, the gene optimization is developed as chromosome (data) which is stored on the CSP. The quality of specific solution is determined by computing the fitness function which in turn find outs the most optimal result from a multiple objective solution in a population. Subsequently, gene based approach is carried out by performing the operations such as selection, crossover and mutation to optimize the multi- objective functions.

The malicious user is detected by analyzing the number of evident (i.e. gens) at every iteration. Normally, each gene has more than one objective functions. By computing the fitness function, the gene is selected based on the information. The fitness function is measured as given below.

$$fitness\ function = identify\ the\ malicious\ user\ based\ on\ multi\ objective\ function \quad \text{.... (4.2)}$$

The proposed GOMOPA technique executes the forensic investigation by considering the objective functions. By utilizing the information of exact evidence which is stored in proof accumulator, the malicious user for specific crime incident is detected on cloud.

The gene operator performs the optimization when the evidence is not admissible to trace the malicious user. After that, the court is confirmed and the malicious user is detected with the evidence of a real suspect.

Selection

In gene optimization, selection process is the first process. The selection process is the process of selecting the most objective function which is determined by the fitness function. Through the selection process, the multi-objective functions are removed which are not optimal.

Crossover

In gene optimization, the crossover operation is performed for swapping the features between two different solutions. The pairs of solutions are used to change the uniqueness which is selected randomly, until an entirely new generation of solution is attained. Based on the objective functions, the mutation operation is performed on the newly generated result which helps to detect the malicious user.

Let us assume, two genes $G_1 =< x_1, x_2, x_3, x_4 >$ and $G_2 =< y_1, y_2, y_3, y_4 >$ with the chromosomes x and y.

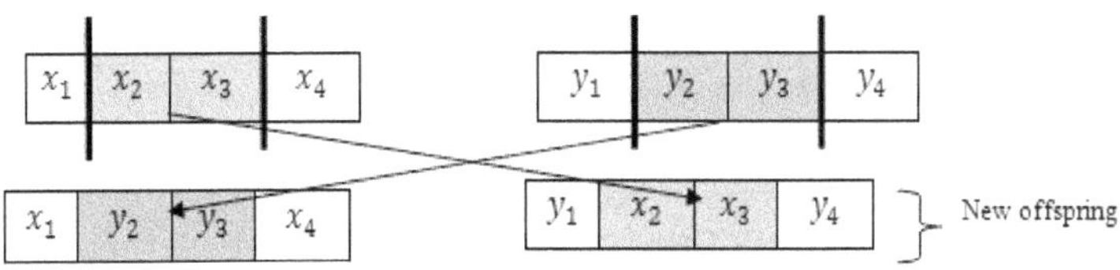

Figure 4.4: Crossover Process

As shown in figure 4.4, the new offspring is generated by performing the recombination process form one point crossover. Based on the high quality chromosomes, the crossover point is selected. After and before the crossover point, the part of chromosomes is swapped to create the new offspring by using parent chromosomes.

Mutation

In gene optimization, mutation operation is performed to exchange some bits of chromosome in a newly generated offspring. The changes obtained in the bits to confirm the evidence with the real suspect to detect the malicious user. Then, the generated offspring are included and the least chromosomes with low fitness values are discarded in the population.

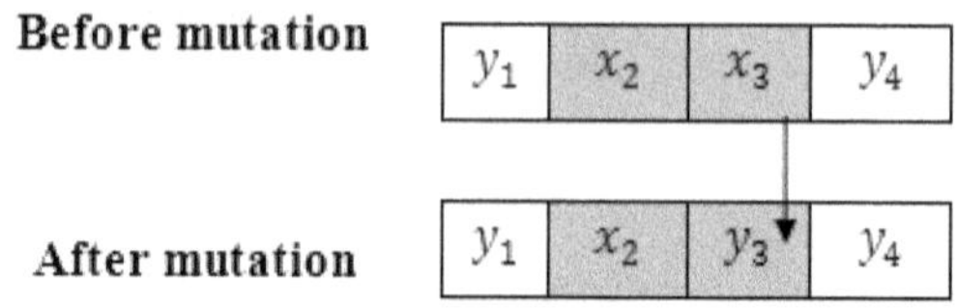

Figure 4.5: Mutation

The above figure 4.5 illustrates the performance of mutation operation to exchange the chromosome value of the gene x_4 with the exact chromosome of y_3. The mutation process is the random exchange of chromosomes to generate the new offspring which improves the fitness function. The newly created offspring is discarded and iterations get repeated when the value of that offspring is less than the fitness threshold.

Input : No. of genes (i.e. evidence), Two parent gene with chromosomes $G1 =< x_1, x_2, x_3, x_4 >$ and $G2 =< y_1, y_2, y_3, y_4 >$

Output : identify the malicious user in cloud

Step 1 : Begin

Step 2: For each investigated evidence

Step 3: Calculate the fitness value

Step 4: if (fitness ≥ threshold) then

Step 5: Number of iteration has been completed and identify the malicious user

Step 6: Selecting more optimized objective function in each iteration

Step 7: Perform crossover operation generates new solution

Step 8: Perform mutation operation

Step 9: Obtain the global optimized solution to identify the malicious user

Step 10: End if

Step 11: End for

Step 12: End

Algorithm 4.1: Gene Optimized Multi-Objective Proof Accumulator Algorithm

Through the mutation process, the local minimum is removed and searched for the global optimal results.

Through the proposed GOMOPA technique, investigated evidence with the real suspect is obtained by CSP to detect the malicious user who launches the malicious activities over the cloud infrastructure. The below algorithm describes the GOMOPA technique to enhance the malicious user identification accuracy with minimum time in cloud forensic environment. The above algorithm 4.1 shows the process of Gene Optimized Multi-objective Proof Accumulator. At first, the gene population generation is started for number of evidence depends on the fitness function with aiming at detecting the malicious user on cloud. Then, the optimal objective functions are selected with specified threshold value through the fitness calculation. The iteration gets finished, when the fitness function is greater than the threshold value. Otherwise, the selection process is performed when the fitness function is less than the threshold value.

Then, the selection process is employed to detect the malicious user with evidence of real suspect which leads to enhance the confidentiality. Then, the crossover process is executed to generate the new optimal solution which is followed by mutation that carries out to discover the exact malicious user. The above process is repeated until the entire evidence is verified. Thereby, the accuracy to identify the malicious user is improved with minimum time.

4.5. Experimental Evaluation of GOMOPA Technique

In this section, the experimental evaluation of proposed Gene Optimized Multi-objective Proof Accumulator (GOMOPA) technique is implemented in java language with CloudSim network simulator.

In order to find out the malicious user with minimal time, the CloudSim simulator uses Amazon EC2 dataset in cloud forensic environment. The CloudSim simulator is performed to ensure the various cloud services with the presented resources and the particular toolkit is utilized as simulation platform in the cloud environment. The performance of proposed GOMOPA technique is compared with existing approach such as Forensic Open-Stack Tools (FROST) by Josiah Dykstra and Alan T. Sherman (2013) and Secure-Logging-as-a-Service (SecLaaS) Scheme by Shams Zawoad et al., (2016) to perform the experiments. The experiments evaluation of proposed GOMOPA technique is carried out on the following metrics such as given below.

- Investigation accuracy,
- Processing time,
- Confidentiality rate.

4.6. Result Analysis of GOMOPA Technique

In order to analysis the efficiency of proposed Gene Optimized Multi-objective Proof Accumulator (GOMOPA) technique which is compared with existing approaches such as Forensic Open-Stack Tools (FROST) by Josiah Dykstra and Alan T. Sherman (2013) and Secure-Logging-as-a-Service (SecLaaS) Scheme by Shams Zawoad et al., (2016). Based on the tables and graph values, the performance of three methods are evaluated along with the following metrics.

4.6.1. Performance Analysis of Investigation Accuracy

The Investigation accuracy is defined as the ratio of the number of malicious users is correctly detected to the total number of cloud users over cloud environment. The mathematical formula for investigation accuracy is measured as follows,

$$Investigation\ accuracy = \frac{(No.of\ cloud\ user - No.of\ malicou\ s\ users)}{Total\ no.of\ cloud\ users} * 100 \quad \text{....Eqn (4.3)}$$

The investigation accuracy is measured in terms of percentage (%). If the investigation accuracy is high, then the technique is said to be more effective.

Table 4.2: Tabulation For Investigation Accuracy

Number of cloud users	Investigation accuracy (%)		
	FROST	SecLaaS scheme	Proposed GOMOPA
10	56.36	64.89	70.06
20	58.72	66.98	72.69
30	60.36	68.89	74.06
40	62.79	70.06	76.06
50	64.46	72.69	78.69
60	66.98	74.06	80.49
70	68.89	76.06	82.87
80	70.06	78.69	84.79
90	72.69	80.49	86.97
100	74.06	82.87	88.96

Above table 4.2 explains the performance of investigation accuracy with respect the different number of cloud users in the cloud environment. To carry out the experiments, the number of cloud user is varied from 10 to 100 which are considered as the input. The above table clearly describes that, the three methods significantly improves the investigation accuracy depending on the number of cloud user.

But comparatively, the better performance of investigation accuracy is achieved by using the proposed GOMOPA technique when compared to other existing approaches such as Forensic Open-Stack Tools (FROST) by Josiah Dykstra and Alan T. Sherman (2013) and Secure-Logging-as-a-Service (SecLaaS) Scheme by Shams Zawoad et al., (2016). Based on the table value, the graph is plotted in below figure 4.6.

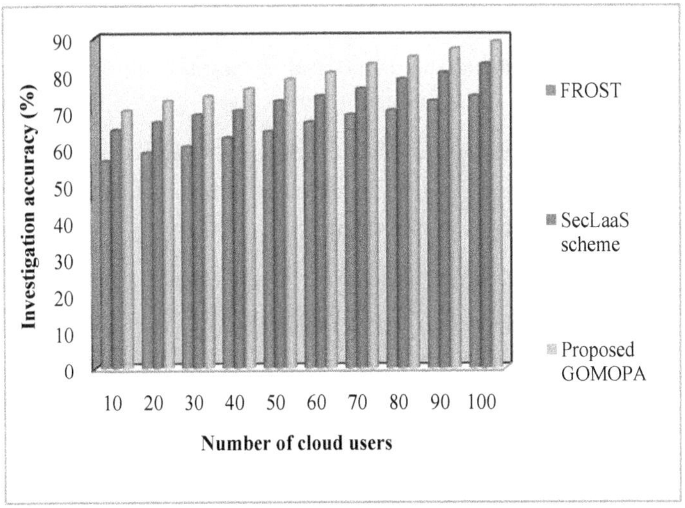

Figure 4.6: Measure of Investigation Accuracy

The figure 4.6 shows the experimental results of investigation accuracy versus number of cloud users which is taken as the range of 10 to 100 for proposed GOMOPA technique which is compared with existing approaches such as Forensic Open-Stack Tools (FROST) and Secure-Logging-as-a-Service (SecLaaS) Scheme. From the figure, it is observed that, the proposed GOMOPA technique ensures improved investigation accuracy to detect the malicious users on cloud than the other existing approaches.

This is because, the proposed GOMOPA technique is developed by using gene based approach which depends on the reporting of multi objective functions as evidence of malicious activities (cloud log files) to the proof accumulator. Then, the proposed GOMOPA technique effectively performs forensic investigation to find out the malicious user. Besides, the optimization of multi objective function using gene optimization enhances the accuracy while investigating the evidences to detect malicious user who initiates the particular crime on cloud infrastructure.

Therefore, the investigation accuracy is improved through the proposed GOMOPA technique up to 22% when compared to the Forensic Open-Stack Tools (FROST) by Josiah Dykstra and Alan T. Sherman (2013) and 8% when compared to the Secure-Logging-as-a-Service (SecLaaS) Scheme.

4.6.2. Performance Analysis of Processing Time

Based on the reports of admissible evidences, the processing time is measured as the amount of time is consumed to identify the malicious user on cloud. The mathematical formula for processing time is measured as follows.

$$Processing\ Time = Number\ of\ cloud\ users * Time\ (identify\ the\ malicious\ user) \quad .... (4.4)$$

The processing time is measured in terms of milliseconds (ms). If the processing time is less, then the technique is said to be more effective.

Table 4.3: Tabulation For Processing Time

Number of cloud users	**Processing time (ms)**		
	FROST	**SecLaaS scheme**	**Proposed GOMOPA**
10	42	36	22
20	44	38	24
30	46	40	26
40	48	42	28
50	50	44	30
60	52	46	32
70	54	48	34
80	56	50	36
90	58	52	38
100	59	54	40

Above table 4.3 explains the performance of processing time with respect the different number of cloud users in the cloud environment.

To conduct the experiments, the number of cloud user is varied from 10 to 100 which are considered as the input. From the table, it is observed that, three methods helps to significantly reduce the processing time depending on the number of cloud user.

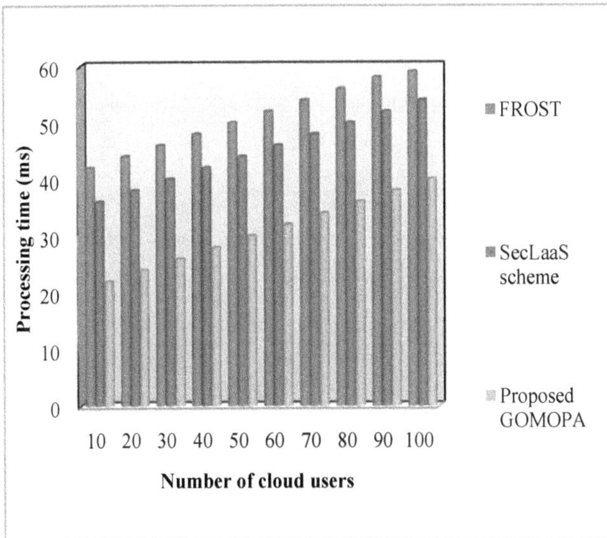

Figure 4.7: Measure of Processing Time

But comparatively, the better performance of processing time is achieved by using the proposed GOMOPA technique when compared to other existing approaches such as Forensic Open-Stack Tools (FROST) by Josiah Dykstra and Alan T. Sherman (2013) and Secure-Logging-as-a-Service (SecLaaS) Scheme by Shams Zawoad et al., (2016). Based on the table value, the graph is plotted in below figure 4.7.The figure 4.7 shows the experimental results of processing time versus number of cloud users which is taken as the range of 10 to 100 for proposed GOMOPA technique which is compared with existing approaches such as Forensic Open-Stack Tools (FROST) and Secure-Logging-as-a-Service (SecLaaS) Scheme. From the figure, it is observed that, the proposed GOMOPA technique consumes less time to process the investigation in order to identify the malicious users on cloud than the other existing approaches. This is because, the proposed GOMOPA technique effectively manages the objective function as time analysis to identify the malicious event occurred in cloud environment. Then, the time information is given to the proof accumulator by the investigator which is followed by the exact malicious user identification with minimized time with the application of gene based approach. Therefore, the processing time is reduced to detect the malicious user by using proposed GOMOPA technique up to 40% when compared to the Forensic Open-Stack Tools (FROST) by Josiah Dykstra and Alan T. Sherman (2013) and 32% when compared to the Secure-Logging-as-a-Service (SecLaaS) Scheme.

4.6.3. *Performance Analysis of Confidentiality Rate*

The confidentiality is the ability of the system to protect the cloud user log files from the unauthorized access in cloud environment. The mathematical formula for confidentiality rate is measured as follows.

$$Confidentiality\ rate = \frac{Number\ \ of\ log\ files\ are\ protected}{Total\ number\ \ of\ cloud\ \log\ files} * 100 \quad \text{....Eqn (4.5)}$$

The confidentiality rate is measured in terms of percentage (%). If the confidentiality rate is high, then the technique is said to be more efficient.

Table 4.4: Tabulation For Confidentiality Rate

Number of cloud log files	**Confidentiality rate (%)**		
	FROST	**SecLaaS scheme**	**Proposed GOMOPA**
5	55.36	63.89	71.06
10	57.72	65.95	73.69
15	59.86	67.89	75.86
20	61.79	69.56	77.49
25	63.46	71.69	79.49
30	65.98	73.06	81.57
35	67.99	75.06	83.79
40	69.06	77.49	85.67
45	71.69	79.69	87.96
50	73.06	81.87	89.96

Above table 4.4 explains the performance of confidentiality rate with respect the different number of cloud log files in the cloud environment. To carry out the experiments, the number of cloud log files is varied from 5 to 50 which are considered as the input. From the table, it is observed that, three methods significantly enhances the confidentiality rate that depends on the number of cloud log files.

But comparatively, the better performance of confidentiality rate is achieved by using the proposed GOMOPA technique when compared to other existing approaches such as Forensic Open-Stack Tools (FROST) by Josiah Dykstra and Alan T. Sherman (2013) and Secure-Logging-as-a-Service (SecLaaS) Scheme by Shams Zawoad et al., (2016). Based on the table value, the graph is plotted in below figure 4.8.

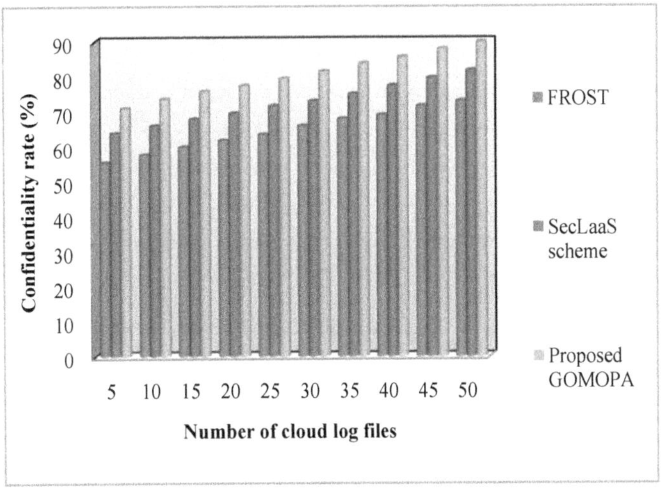

Figure 4.8: Measure of Confidentiality Rate

The figure 4.8 shows the experimental results for confidentiality rate versus number of cloud log files which is taken as the range of 5 to 50 for proposed GOMOPA technique that is compared with existing approaches such as Forensic Open-Stack Tools (FROST) and Secure-Logging-as-a-Service (SecLaaS) Scheme. From the figure, it is observed that, the proposed GOMOPA technique achieves higher confidentiality rate while investigating the evidences of malicious activities to find out the malicious user on cloud than the other existing approaches.

This is because, the multiple cloud log files are protected from unauthorized access with the help of proposed GOMOPA technique while reporting the multi-objective functions as evidence of malicious users by investigator to the proof accumulator. Thereby the investigation accuracy is improved which leads to enhance the confidentiality. In addition, gene based approach validates the investigated evidence of cloud log file with real suspect by CSP to estimate the optimal solution. From that, the privacy level gets improved that guarantees the confidentiality. Therefore, confidentiality rate is improved up to 25% by proposed GOMOPA technique when compared to the Forensic Open-Stack Tools (FROST) by Josiah Dykstra and Alan T. Sherman (2013) and 11% when compared to the Secure-Logging-as-a-Service (SecLaaS) Scheme.

4.7. Summary

An efficient Gene Optimized Multi-objective Proof Accumulator (GOMOPA) technique is developed to recognize the malicious user on cloud by reporting the acceptable evidence to the proof accumulator. At first, the multi-objective functions as evidence of malicious activities are reported to the proof accumulator by the cloud forensic investigator. Subsequently, these objective functions are optimized by implementing the gene based approach. Based on the fitness function, the gene based approach find outs optimal solution to identify the user who initiates malicious activities. When the evidence is not accepted by the accumulator, the gene operations such as selection, crossover and mutation are carried out for detection of malicious users with the evidence of real suspect. During the gene operations, the confidentiality of cloud log files is achieved on cloud.

Moreover, the performance of proposed GOMOPA technique is verified with the metrics such as investigation accuracy, processing time and confidentiality rate by Amazon EC2 dataset with CloudSim simulator. The experiments results show that the proposed GOMOPA technique detects the malicious users with improvement of investigation accuracy and confidentiality rate up to 15% and 18% by implementing the gene optimization approach. By submitting the multi-objective functions to the proof accumulator, the processing time is minimized by 36% for discovering the malicious user on cloud environment. Finally, the malicious user with evidence of real suspect is detected with the application of proposed GOMOPA technique by observing their activities. In addition, the Spatiotemporal Forensic Data Collector and Swarm Optimized Multi-Objective Proof Accumulator (SFDC-SOMOPA) technique is implemented in order to guarantee the security for the cloud user's data on cloud infrastructure. The proposed SFDC-SOMOPA technique is performed with Spatiotemporal Forensic Data Collector, Fault tolerant Time Synchronization method and Watershed Forensic Logging Filter to provide better secure cloud services while detecting the malicious users which is briefly described in the forthcoming chapter.

CHAPTER V

SPATIOTEMPORAL FORENSIC DATA COLLECTION AND ISOLATION BASED PARTICLE SWARM OPTIMIZATION FOR SECURED CLOUD SERVICES

5.1. Introduction

In cloud computing, the forensic investigator offers the secured cloud services to many users at a time. In the cloud forensic investigation, the forensic data (evidence of malicious user) is collected from cloud server and then examined, analyzed and reported to detect the exact malicious user who launches the malicious activities on cloud environment. Some of techniques were developed to recognize the malicious user through the cloud forensic analysis. The secure provenance scheme was implemented with the objective of achieving the confidentiality on stored data documents in cloud. Then, the security as a service model was developed to prevent the cloud infrastructure by ensuring the baseline security to the provider. In addition, the Secure-Logging-as-a-Service (SecLaaS) scheme was developed with the aim of achieving the confidentiality and integrity to the produce logs for events of virtual machines. But, these techniques need to be enhanced for providing accurate results cause for crime incident.

In previous chapter, the evidence of malicous actions for crime incident is identified through the Spatio-Temporal Forensic Data Collector and Logging filter (STFDC-LF) technique. Followed by, Gene Optimized Multi-objective Proof Accumulator (GOMOPA) technique that detects the malicious user based on the multi objectives optimized by proof accumulator. Though these techniques are used to find out the malicious user for crime event, the privacy of normal user and security of the data access not effectively provided. In order to find out exact malicious user with better confidentiality rate, the Spatiotemporal Forensic Data Collector and Swarm Optimized Multi-Objective Proof Accumulator (SFDC-SOMOPA) technique is proposed in this chapter.

The integaration of Spatiotemporal Forensic Data Collector and Swarm Optimized Multi-Objective Proof Accumulator (SFDC-SOMOPA) technique is introduced with the aim of achieving the secured cloud services on cloud environment. The malicious user is detected with admissible evidence by performing the proposed SFDC-SOMOPA technique with three processes. Initially, through the Spatiotemporal Forensic Data Collector, the multiple users of cloud log files are acquired from various cloud resources related with physical location and the temporal information.

Then, the Fault tolerant Time Synchronization method is used to extract the precise time for detecting the evidence of malicious activities. Secondly, the Watershed Forensic Logging Filter (WFLF) is introduced to assure the data privacy by isolating the log files of the multiple cloud users.

Finally, Swarm Optimized Multi-objective Proof Accumulator (SOMOPA) is developed to submit the evidence with multi objective functions into proof accumulator. Then, the particle swarm optimization is performed to detect the exact malicious user depending on the fitness calculation. As a result, through the proposed SFDC-SOMOPA technique, the malicious user with real suspect is detected, who launches the malicious activities over the cloud infrastructure, and thereby the confidentiality of the cloud users' log files is improved.

5.2. Secure Provenance Scheme

According to the group signature and attribute-based signature techniques, Jin Li et al., (2014) developed a new secure provenance scheme to guarantee the confidentiality while storing perceptive documents, forming a provenance record, authenticating the cloud servers and ensuring the fine-grained access control on documents in cloud environment.

In cloud computing, the secure provenance scheme was introduced with the objective of considering the two main issues related with fine-grained access control and low computation and communication overhead at the data owner or user side in cloud. Through the secure provenance scheme, the privacy of cloud user was ensured over a cloud platform. The cloud is involved with the four security requirements such as confidentiality, unforgeability, anonymity and traceability for providing the secure provenance system.

In cloud environment, the provenance system was developed with five entities such as data owners, data users, cloud server, attribute authorities and third-party auditor. Initially, the data owner stores their perceptive data on the cloud server. Besides, the data owner was permitted to run their own code and to access their sensitive data on the cloud server. Then, the user's attributes private keys were obtained by cloud users from the attribute authorities with the help of anonymous key-issuing protocol which protects the user privacy.

There was necessary for cloud users to provide their access privilege to the cloud server, in order to access and manage the remote saved data documents which were shared on cloud server by data owner. By moving the user access to the cloud server, the computation and communication overhead for the data owner was reduced. The cloud server was online state for all time which was controlled by the Cloud Service Provider (CSP). The cloud server contained with abundant storage capability and computation power.

Then, the identity of malicious (dishonest) user was discovered through the third-party auditor while handling the documents in a different manner from other normal users. However, the secure provenance scheme was not sufficient enough to perform the investigation for effectively minimizing the data owner's communication overhead on cloud environment.

5.3. Security as A Service Model

In cloud infrastructure, Vijay Varadharajan and Udaya Tupakula (2014) introduce security as a service model to cloud service provider for ensuring a security to its tenants and customers of its tenants. Different attacks such as insider attack from tenant domain and cloud service provider, denial of service attacks were detected through the security as a service model. The security architecture was presented by providing the security as a service model for cloud provider to guarantee as a part of its infrastructure to its customers (tenants) aiming at addressing the above mentioned attacks.

The security architecture was implemented with components such as Host Based Security Tools (HBST), Service Provider Attack Detection (SPAD) and Tenant Specific Attack Detection (TSAD). The HBST was provided by the cloud service provider to the cloud user. Then, the cloud customer may wish to have their own tools HBST for running the virtual machines.

From that, HBST ensures the primary layer of defense to the cloud architecture. The SPAD provides the security baseline policy that was needed to the cloud service provider. Then, the TSAD assures the tenant specific attack detection policies on cloud architecture. However, it offers security to the cloud architecture and flexibility to the tenants but it easily adopts the number of security and compliance issues.

5.4. Secure-Logging-As-A-Service (SECLAAS) Scheme

In cloud environment, Shams Zawoad et al., (2016) introduces the Secure-Logging-as-a-Service (SecLaaS) scheme to provide good results for achieving the confidentiality and integrity for generated log to analyze the activity of virtual machines.With the application of SecLaaS scheme, the cloud log files were collected from various resources such as network, process, and databases in a secured manner to detect the malicious user on cloud environment.

Then, the CSP or investigator was prevented from unauthorized access by introducing the Proof of Past Log (PPL) as a tamper evident scheme. Besides, the variation of Bloom filter scheme was introduced for presenting the security than the traditional Bloom filter approach.

Initially, the various cloud log files were extracted from Node Controller (NC) for each VM. After that, the log database stores the extracted log files. From that, the log files were utilized to form log database for performing the investigation even if the VM was terminated. While storing the logs into the log database, the integrity and confidentiality of the logs were ensured with the application of SecLaaS scheme. Then, the SecLaaS scheme prevents the access of proof to that log from proof database. From the specific IP, the required logs were discovered through the API by the investigator. Then, the accepted i.e. exact evidence of malicious user was provided by analyzing the proofs of past logs along with the logs which ensures the secured service in cloud. However, it difficult to decrease the investigation time in the cloud infrastructure.

5.5. Spatiotemporal Forensic Data Collector And Swarm Optimized Multi-Objective Proof Accumulator (SFDC-SOMOPA) Technique

In cloud environment, the cloud forensic investigation is the digital forensic procedure which contained different process such as data collection, examination, analysis and reporting the forensic data to preserve the privacy of information and confidentiality. The cloud forensic contains legal, technical and organizational suggestions which are depending on each other while performing the investigation process on cloud environment.

Due to the complexity and invisibility of cloud architecture, the collection of admissible evidences of the malicious user from cloud systems by investigator becomes a major concern in order to perform the forensic investigation in some criminal cases.

Therefore, an efficient integrated technique called as Spatiotemporal Forensic Data Collector and Swarm Optimized Multi-Objective Proof Accumulator (SFDC-SOMOPA) technique is introduced for performing cloud forensic analysis on cloud forensic data. Through the proposed SFDC-SOMOPA technique, the evidences of malicious activities are collected from cloud server and the real admissible evidences are reported to the proof accumulator with the aim of proving the crime activities inside the cloud environment. The architectural diagram of the proposed SFDC-SOMOPA technique is described in the following figure 5.1.

As shown in figure 5.1, the exact malicious user who initiates the crime on cloud is identified by implementing the Spatiotemporal Forensic Data Collector and swarm Optimized Multi-Objective Proof Accumulator (SFDC-SOMOPA) technique in cloud forensic analysis. In order to ensure secured cloud services, the proposed SFDC-SOMOPA technique is carried out in three steps. At first, different cloud log files are obtained from various resources for extracting the evidence of malicious activities inside the cloud environment.

In this step, the Spatiotemporal Forensic Data Collector and Fault tolerant Time Synchronization are developed to discover the time of crime activities. Secondly, Watermarked Forensic logging filter (WFLF) is introduced to separate the cloud log files of the multiple cloud users which lead to preserve the data privacy of cloud users from the malicious users.

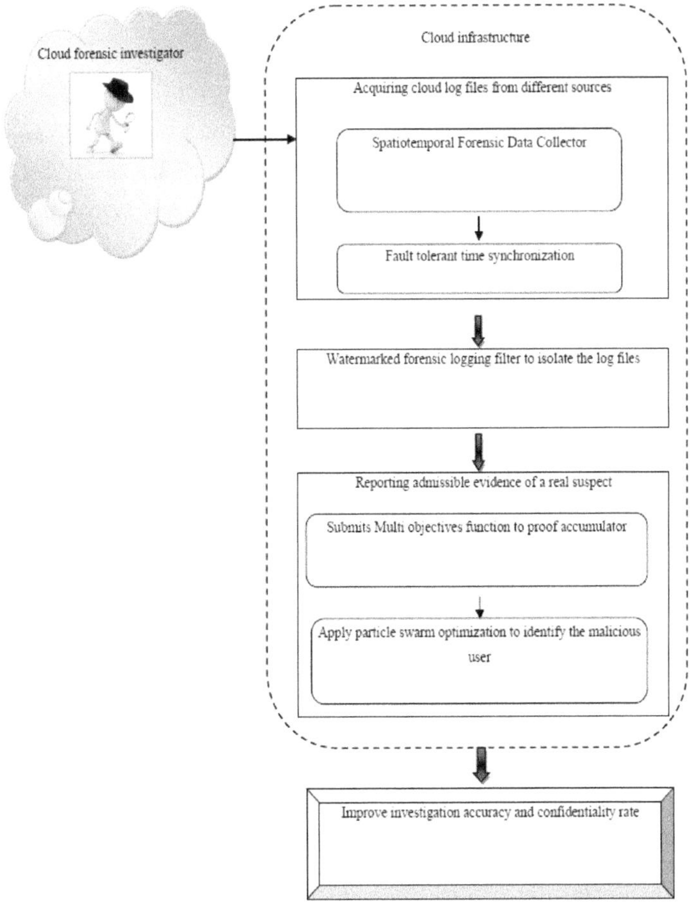

Figure 5.1: Architecture diagram of the Spatiotemporal Forensic Data Collector and swarm Optimized Multi-objective Proof Accumulator

In third step, particle swarm optimization is introduced to find out the accurate malicious user who launches the crime on cloud infrastructure. Then, the cloud log files which are saved in Virtual Machine (VM) are verified by Cloud Service Provider (CSP).

After that, the cloud forensic investigator submits multi-objective functions such as integrity, data possession, provenance information, time stamp information and location information into a proof accumulator. Subsequently, the particle swarm optimization is developed to discover the exact malicious user by identifying global best optimal solution (i.e. evidence) thereby the investigation accuracy and confidentiality rate are improved. The brief explanation of the SFDC-SOMOPA technique is obtained in following subsections.

5.5.1. Collection of Cloud Log Files From Various Sources

The acquiring of cloud log files from various sources like application logs, storage logs, computing logs, and network logs is the first process in the design of proposed SFDC-SOMOPA technique. The cloud log files of particular VM resource are obtained by the proposed SFDC-SOMOPA technique. The obtained cloud log files hold the reliable evidence to the malicious activities. Therefore, the Spatiotemporal Forensic Data Collector and Fault tolerant Time Synchronization are applied in the proposed SFDC-SOMOPA technique to acquire the cloud log files from different sources.

5.5.1.1.Spatiotemporal Forensic Data Collector

In proposed SFDC-SOMOPA technique, Spatiotemporal Forensic Data Collector is developed to discover the exact time and location of crime event occurred in the cloud environment. The Spatiotemporal Forensic Data Collector is a database which manages information about both location and time against the evidential artifacts by activity logs in the cloud. The Spatiotemporal Forensic Data Collector is used in some criminal cases to extract the forensic data which is related with particular location at a specified time of crime event.

Let us assume, the 'L' denotes the location where the data to be collected. The location contains more regions $r_1, r_2, r_3, \ldots, r_n$. Each region comprises of the number of spatial objects $O_{1,}O_2, O_3 \ldots O_n$ with a time intervals $\{t_1, t_{2,}t_3, \ldots . t_n\}$. Then, the cloud log files are collected which is related with location and time. Each user in cloud collects the continuous data (n) samples among the time interval T which is formulated as follows,

$$CU_i = \{u_i^1, u_i^2, \ldots u_i^n\} \quad \text{....Eqn (5.1)}$$

From the above equation (5.1), continuous data (1, 2, 3... n) are collected by the cloud users$\{u_i^1, u_i^2, \ldots u_i^n\}$. With the help of global weighted vector, spatiotemporal data is restored in a cyclical order within a particular interval of time through the proposed SFDC-SOMOPA technique which is formulated as given below.

$$D_i = u_i W_o + V_i \quad \text{....Eqn (5.2)}$$

From the equation 5.2, the corresponding data is stored in cloud server which is denoted by D_i, the initial weighted vector of cloud users (u_i) is denoted by W_o and the spatial and temporal uncorrelated data is denoted by V_i. The correlation of spatiotemporal data between the cloud users and servers is obtained by using Spatiotemporal Data Collector. From that, Spatiotemporal Data Collector does not require any prior knowledge about the data and it has the tracing capability to observe the internal variation of the cloud environments.

Then, the global statistical information (i.e. evident) is collected related with the crime incident by cloud server which is evaluated as given below.

$$R_{uu} = E[UU^T] = \begin{bmatrix} E[u_1 u_1] \dots \dots . E[u_1 u_m] \\ \vdots \\ E[u_m u_1] \dots \dots E[u_m u_{m1}] \end{bmatrix} \quad \text{....Eqn (5.3)}$$

$$R_{Du} = E(DU) = \begin{bmatrix} E\ [Du_1] \\ E\ [Du_2] \\ \cdot\cdot \\ \cdot\cdot \\ E[Du_M] \end{bmatrix} \quad \text{....Eqn (5.4)}$$

From the above equation (5.3), (5.4), R_{uu} and R_{Du} represents the Two global statistical information. Here, the covariance of the matrix 'U' is represented as E. Hence, the global weighted vector at the cloud server is measured as given below.

$$W_l^G = W_{l-1}^G + \mu \sum_{i=1}^{m} (R_{Du,l} - R_{uu} W_{l-1}) \quad \text{....Eqn (5.5)}$$

From the above equation (5.5), the current global weighted vector is denoted as W_l^G, the previous global weighted vector is denoted as W_{l-1}^G and the positive step size parameter is denoted as μ. For each server, the newly updated vector is computed as given below.

$$W_{i,l}^N = W_{i,l-1} + \mu \left(u_i^T \left(D_i^N - u_i W_{i,l-1} \right) \right) \quad \text{....Eqn (5.6)}$$

From the above equation (5.6), the new updated weight vector data (D_i^N) with multiple users is represented as $W_{i,l}^N$ and the user's login time is represented as u_i^T. In order to collect the evidence about crime event, the statistical information of each cloud user is obtained by newly updated weight vector. Then, the user is detected as malicious user, when the statistical information of the user is varied from the normal users. During the forensic investigation, the malicious user provides the incorrect data information thereby the location and crime time of malicious activities is detected with the help of Spatiotemporal Forensic Data Collector.

5.5.1.2. Fault Tolerant Time Synchronization

The proposed SFDC-SOMOPA technique is implemented with Fault tolerant time synchronization on the acquired cloud log files of a specific crime event.

Synchronization is the process of ensuring the set of cloud log files to complete a task with accurate runtime. The timestamp comprises necessary information if the event is happening on the cloud environment. Each event contains time stamp which helps to report the time after the record was generated. The synchronization of time event is considered as source of evidence while analyzing the cloud log files on cloud infrastructure.

The dynamic nature of cloud structure is more prone to failure. Hence, fault tolerance plays significant role on cloud infrastructure in order to ensure the reliability in the real time computing. In cloud environment, reliability of the system ensures the failure-free service for a specific time periods. In cloud computing, various kinds of faults can occurred, such as network fault, CPU fault, memory fault, Fault in storage, Power failure and process faults. Hence, through the proposed SFDC-SOMOPA technique, these faults are tolerated for enhancing the reliability. The Fault tolerant time synchronization technique enables VM to prolong the operation properly in the failure of some of its components which leads to ensure the reliable cloud computing system. The figure 5.2 shows the Fault tolerant time in cloud environment.

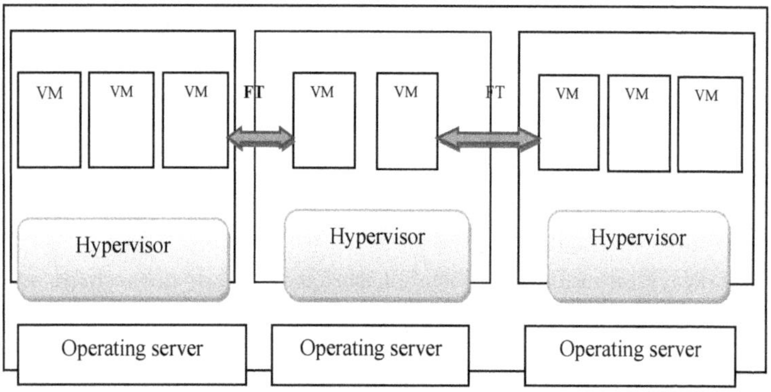

Figure 5.2: Fault Tolerant in Cloud Environment

As shown in figure 5.2, VMs keeps the operation properly to minimize the error rate through the fault tolerant on cloud. The hypervisor runs a number of virtual machines (VM) known as host machine. Each virtual machine is considered as a guest machine. Generally, the fault tolerant is managed by two approaches such as reactive fault tolerance and proactive fault tolerance. The reactive fault tolerance approach is used to decrease the results of failures while running an application. The proactive fault tolerance approach removes the recovery from faults, error and failures by identifying them. Then, the proactive fault tolerance approach is used to proactively modify the uncertain elements into other operational components.

Hence, providing effective result as certain level of time synchronization is achieved with the help of proactive fault tolerance approach. In addition, the proactive fault tolerance approach tolerates the faults and generates the decision depends on the reliability of virtual machines.

In cloud environment, the proposed SFDC-SOMOPA technique improves the reliability by using the adaptive fault tolerance technique. The figure 5.3 shows the processing diagram of the adaptive fault tolerance.

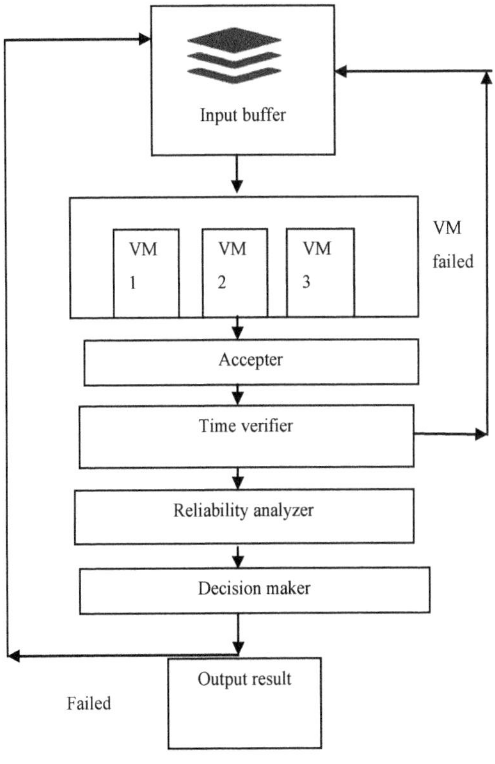

Figure 5.3: Processing Diagram of the Adaptive Fault Tolerance

As shown in figure 5.3, the better results are achieved through the adaptive fault tolerance. The cloud environment contains number of Virtual Machines (VMs). In cloud, each VM collects the input data from the input buffer. Then, this collected input is passed to the entire VMs to run different operations. From that, the input data is taken by each VM to carry out some operations which provide better results.

Then, the produced results are forwarded to the accepter unit and then it checks the VMs for all iterations. The accepter unit does not send any information to the Time verifier, when the testing result is not accurate. Otherwise, the accepter unit forwards the information to the Time verifier for decision result and reliability evaluation, if the testing result is correct.

In cloud, the Time verifier set the time for each VM. In addition, Time verifier is used to observe the timing results and to check whether the accurate output was created at the specific amount of time limit or not. The Time verifier forwards only an accurate result of those VM that creates results before the deadline time. In cloud environment, the internal clock of VMs and any of the virtual resources are maintained by CSP which also controls the physical machines synchronization. In addition, the CSP manages their clocks to comprise for an accurate time. The time synchronization in cloud is ensured among virtual machines through the Network Time Protocol.

In cloud platform, the reliability is computed for each VM through the reliability analyzer. The reliability of the VM is varied for every computing cycle. Initially, the reliability is 100% for each VM. The reliability of VM is improved when the exact result is generated by VM within the time limit. Otherwise, the reliability of VM gets decreased. In cloud, for maximum and minimum reliability, each VM contained predefined limit value. Hence, the reliability is referred as the probability of the system to work correctly. The reliability is the ability of the system to ensure necessary function under definite conditions within a prescribed time interval. The mathematical formula for reliability of a service is computed as given follows.

$$Reliability = \frac{successful\ responce\ from\ cloud}{Total\ request\ from\ users} * 100 \quad ....\text{Eqn } (5.7)$$

At last, the decision maker is utilized for computing cycle by identifying the final output results. Through the decision maker, the output of VM is discovered which holds the highest reliability among all the VMs. The VM which has minimum reliability is removed and then new one is added. According to the priority (which VM has the highest priority), the VM is selected if the two VM have similar reliability. In cloud, the selection of VM plays the significant task which ensures correct results within a required time. Then, the adaptive fault tolerance is carried out to produce accurate output results until all the VM fail. Hence, the proposed SFDC-SOMOPA technique ensures enhanced output results in the fault tolerance and time synchronization.

5.5.2. Isolation of Cloud Log Files

The isolation of cloud log files by using Watermarked forensic logging filter is the second process in the design of proposed SFDC-SOMOPA technique.

The isolation is the important process for discovering the particular types of log information and reorganizing them by time, IP address, User ID, and so on.

The multiple cloud users log data are contained with the recovered cloud log files of VM resources. In proposed SFDC-SOMOPA technique, the cloud log files of multiple cloud users are isolated with the help of Watershed forensic logging filter (WFLF). Thereby, the data privacy of the malicious users and other cloud users is preserved on cloud environment. The Watermarked forensic logging filter is concentrated on the unique user ID, and specific event of the temporally retrieved log files to separate the cloud log files. Based on the event happened in cloud, the log files are isolated which contains the information unrelated to the crime event through the Watermarked forensic logging filter. Concurrently, Watermarked forensic logging filter achieves the better confidentiality of the multiple cloud users who shares the similar cloud infrastructure. As a result, the evidence of cloud log files (malicious) is controlled by labeling the malicious activities with the application of proposed SFDC-SOMOPA technique.

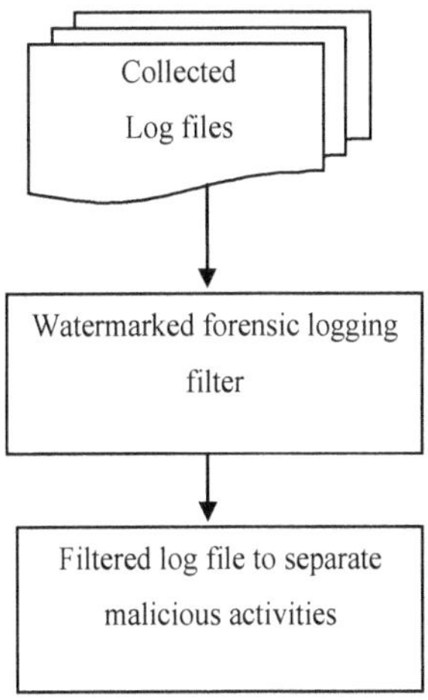

Figure 5.4: Process of Watermarked Forensic Logging Filter

As shown in figure 5.4, the malicious activities of multiple cloud log files are isolated by using Watermarked Forensic logging Filter. For each malicious user, the markers are assigned to isolate them from normal users. The watermark is the piece of information such as User-ID is implanted in the markers without corrupting the log files that helps to verify the evidence. The sequences of events from different logs are generated by sending the collected log files which is taken as input to the monitoring framework.

Then, with the application of Spearman rank correlation, the degree of association between the events is discovered for isolating the log files which are normal or malicious. The mathematical formula for Spearman rank correlation is measured as given below.

$$\rho = cor\ (e_1 e_2) = 1 - \frac{6 \sum d_i^2}{n(n^2-1)} \quad ....\text{Eqn (5.8)}$$

From the above equation (5.8), the difference between the rank of two events of tenants is denoted as 'd_i', the number of cloud users $u_1, u_2, .. u_n$ is denoted as 'n', the correlation coefficient is denoted as ρ and occurred events in cloud are denoted as $e_1 e_2$. The positive correlation '1' is provided by the perfect Spearman correlation coefficient if the evaluated two events are related to detect the malicious activities. Otherwise, the negative correlation '-1' is provided by perfect Spearman correlation coefficient if the two events are not related to detect the malicious activities. Based on the correlation measure, the cloud log files are identified which are related and unrelated to the crime incident. Through the filtering techniques, the cloud log files are identified which are related to malicious activities. In cloud environment, the malicious user and other user are discovered by using correlation filtering approach. After filtering the log files of malicious user, watermarking is used to isolate the filtered log files. The watermarking assigns the markers for each malicious user other than the normal users thereby the data privacy to the normal users gets improved with the help of Watermarked Forensic logging Filter algorithm which is described as follows.

Input: Number of cloud users '$CU_i = u_1, u_2, .. u_n$', Spearman correlation coefficient 'ρ'

Output: Isolate the cloud log files

Step 1: **Begin**

Step 2: **For** each events of tenants

Step 3: Calculate the Spearman rank correlation coefficient using (5.8)

Step 4: If(positive correlation '+1')

Step 5: Identify log files related to malicious activities

Step 6: else If (negative correlation '-1')

Step 7: Identify log files related to normal activities

Step 8: **End if**

Step 9: Isolate the malicious log files by assigning the marker

Step 10: **End for**

Step 11: **End**

Algorithm 5.1: Watermarked Forensic Logging Filter

The above figure 5.1 illustrates the Watermarked Forensic logging Filter algorithm to identify and isolate the malicious activities related or unrelated to the crime incident. The Spearman rank correlation coefficient is computed for each event of tenants. Then, the cloud log file is taken as related to the crime event, when the coefficient ensures positive correlation '+1'. Otherwise, the cloud log file is taken as unrelated to the crime event, when the coefficient ensures negative correlation '-1'. Later, through the watermarking, the cloud logs files related with crime event are separated by assigning the marker to detect the all possible unauthorized access. The watermarking forensic logging filter is used to separate the log files of the multiple cloud users and ensure the admissible forensic evidence to the malicious activity. This in turns, the data privacy of the malicious users and other cloud users are provided. Subsequently, the acquired and separated proof of malicious activities is reported to the proof accumulator to detect the exact malicious users which are described in following sections.

5.5.3. Submission of Admissible Evidence

After the isolation of cloud log files of malicious activites, these files are submitted by the forensic investigator. In additon, the multiple objective functions such as evidence of integrity, provenance information, data possession evidence, and time stamp information also reported into a proof accumulator. In proposed SFDC-SOMOPA technique, CSP validates the investigated evidence with the evidence of a real suspect to determine the malicious user on cloud infrastructure.

5.5.3.1. Analysis of Multi Objective Functions

The proposed SFDC-SOMOPA technique analysis the multi-objective functions of malicious cloud user activities, proof of integrity, provenance information, proof of data possession, time stamp and location information to detect the exact malicious user. The multi-objective functions are briefly explained as follows.

The integrity assures that the accuracy of evidence over its complete progress. The integrity is retained by listing the events in chain of custody register which comprises such as how, where and who launches the malicious activities over the cloud infrastructure. The chain of custody register aids to accept the evidence by court of law. In the forensic analysis, the maintenance of chain of custody is the important for specific criminal cases.

The Provable Data Possession (PDP) possesses the proof of data possession for validating whether the investigator obtained the real evidence or not to detect the malicious user. Then, this evidence is reported to the multi objective proof accumulator.

In cloud environment, the cloud user forwards the file into a server and generates the new log files with the creation of data possession. The CSP is recognized with the storage information of specific user, after updating the file into a server. In order to ensure secured cloud service provisioning with better confidentiality, the CSP stores the log files with the help of tiger hash storage. For each user, the CSP recovers the tiger hash entry at the end of the day.

In forensic analysis, Data Provenance information is the essential objective function for demonstrating the history of digital evidence and preventing the records integrity. The Data Provenance information contains review, date and time of the event occurs, specific user ID and the information about the activities performed on the source data. In addition, the Data Provenance information ensures information about where and when the action is happening over a cloud which leads to guarantee the confidentiality and removes the repudiation.

In cloud environment, the timestamp is one of the important objective function to extract the time of event happened. The timestamp includes date, time of day, and small fraction of a second. The time of evidence is detected by delivering the proof of data possession gradually. It may be either accurate generation time or a time range in which the event is occurred. Each evidences contained with stamp, time field and report of the evidence time. After that, the location of the crime event is discovered.

With the applicaion of particle swarm optimization and with the collected evidence, these objective functions are optimized to find out the malicious user with exact evidence.

5.5.3.2. Identification of Malicious User

The Particle Swarm Optimization (PSO) offers the population of multiple objective functions that ensures the confidentiality to achieve the optimal solutions at every generation. The optimization is the process of obtaining the best evidence to confirm the crime activities and discover the malicious user with real suspect.

The Swarm Optimized Multi-Objective Proof Accumulator (SOMOPA) optimizes the objective functions with the aim of discovering set of most relevant evidence by initializing the population (i.e. multiple objective functions or swarm) and constraints. From that, through the accurate fitness assignment, the optimal solution is attained.

The particles are considered as candidate solutions (i.e. evidence) while performing the PSO. Each particle contained with position and velocity and is also recognized with their best position. Based on the available evidence of realities, the velocity and position are discovered.

Let us assume, the number of particles (i.e. $i = 1,..,n$) are distributed in the swarm and the position of particle is represented as P_i^k. Based on the velocity V_i^k to the current position, the position of particle is altered. Then, the position of the particles is computed as follows.

$$P_i^{k+1} = P_i^k + V_i^{k+1} \quad \text{....Eqn (5.9)}$$

As shown in above equation (5.9), according to the current position of the particles P_i^k and adjusted velocity V_i^{k+1} , the updated position of particle P_i^{k+1} is computed. Therefore, the velocity of the particle is updated which is expressed as follows,

$$V_i^{k+1} = W_t V_i^k + c_1 r_1 * (pbest_i - P_i^k) + C_2 r_2 (gbest - P_i^k) \quad \text{....Eqn (5.10)}$$

As shown in above equation (5.10), the particle velocity for iteration 'k' is represented as V_i^k, the particle velocity for iteration 'k+1' is represented as V_i^{k+1}, the position of current particle is represented as P_i^k.

Here, the random number between 0 and 1 is denoted as $r_{1,}r_2$, the acceleration factors are denoted as $c1, c2$ and weight factor is denoted as W_t .Every particle is commune with subset of all particles, which is referred as its position of the particle (local best i.e. Pbest). In the population, the position of particles is denoted as gbest. The current position of particles is updated, while updating the position and velocity of each particle.

The global best of its entire population is determined for all iteration to discover the malicious user. Every particle in PSO contains fitness value to control the collection of the log files. According to the multiple objective functions, the fitness function is computed which expressed as follows.

$$fitness\ function\ (F) = identify\ the\ malicious\ user\ based\ on\ multi\ objective\ function \quad \text{....Eqn (5.11)}$$

From the above equation (5.11), based on the fitness function the malicious user is identified. Hence, with the help of optimal evidence information in proof accumulator, the malicious user is detected. Each particle verifies the fitness with their population.

The fitness value is greater than the best fitness value (pbest) and then the current fitness value is fixed as new pbest. In the population, the particle is set as global best (gbest) which has the best fitness value.

Then, the particles with best fitness value are selected as exact evidence for determining the malicious user. The below algorithm describes the swarm optimized multi objective proof accumulator algorithm.

Input : Number of particles $i = 1,..,n$, Acceleration factors 'C1, C2', weighting factor 'W_t', Random number $r_{1,}r_2$

Output : Identify the malicious user in cloud

Step 1: **Begin**

Step 2: Initialize the particles position and velocity in a random manner

Step 3: For each particle

Step 4: **Do**

Step 4: Calculate fitness function using (5.11)

Step 5: If (fitness function > $pbest$) then

Step 6: Set the current fitness value as the $pbest$

Step 7: end if

Step 8: If ($pbest$>gbest) then

Step 7: Select the particle with the best fitness value in the population set as the $gbest$

Step 8: end if

Step 9: Update particle position using (5.9)

Step 10: Calculate velocity of the particle using (5.10)

Step 11: While (maximum iteration is not met)

Step 12: End for

Step 13: End

Algorithm 5.2: Swarm Optimized Multi-Objective Proof Accumulator Algorithm

As shown in algorithm 5.2, the exact malicious user is discovered through the Swarm Optimized Multi-objective Proof Accumulator algorithm by validating the multi-objective functions with the evidence of a real suspect. At first, the swarm population generation is started for number of evidence to detect the malicious user.

Then, the fitness values are computed for all evidences to select the optimal objective function.

The current fitness value is set as pbest, if the fitness value is greater than the current fitness. From that, the particle which has the best fitness value is identified and set as global best (i.e. gbest) among the populations.

Based on the updating of the position of particles, the velocity of the particles is determined for all iteration, until the entire evidence is verified. Thereby the exact malicious user with minimal time is discovered.

5.6. Experimental Evaluation SFDC-SOMOPA Technique

The Spatiotemporal Forensic Data Collector and Swarm Optimized Multi-Objective Proof Accumulator (SFDC-SOMOPA) technique is implemented by using CloudSim network simulator. In cloud environment, the Amazon access sample dataset is used by CloudSim simulator to detect the malicious users.

The Amazon access sample dataset is obtained from the UCI repository. Then, the Amazon access sample dataset contains 4 types of attributes such as Person_Attribute, Resource_ID, Group_ID and System_Support_ID. In cloud platform, the CloudSim simulator is carried out to offer different services with the accessible resources and the particular toolkit which taken as a simulation platform. During cloud forensic investigation, the malicious user is detected with minimum time through the Cloudsim.

The experiments are carried out to evaluate the performance of proposed Spatiotemporal Forensic Data Collector and Swarm Optimized Multi-Objective Proof Accumulator (SFDC-SOMOPA) technique which is compared with the existing methods such as Secure provenance scheme, Security as a Service Model and Secure-Logging-as-a-Service (SecLaaS) Scheme. The evaluation of proposed SFDC-SOMOPA technique is conducted on the following factors as given below.

- Investigation accuracy,
- Investigation time,
- Filtering efficiency,
- Processing time and
- Confidentiality rate.

5.7. Result Analysis of SFDC-SOMOPA Technique

The result analysis of the proposed Spatiotemporal Forensic Data Collector and Swarm Optimized Multi-Objective Proof Accumulator (SFDC-SOMOPA) technique is carried out with existing methods such as Secure Provenance Scheme by Jin Li et al., (2014), Security as a Service Model by Vijay Varadharajan and Udaya Tupakula (2014) and Secure-Logging-as-a-Service (SecLaaS) Scheme by Shams Zawoad et al., (2016). Based on the tables and graph values, the performance of three methods are estimated along with the following metrics.

5.7.1. Performance Analysis of Investigation Accuracy

The Investigation accuracy is measured as the ratio of number of malicious user accurately identified to the total number of cloud users in the cloud environment.

When the investigation accuracy is high, then the technique is said to be more efficient. The Investigation accuracy is measured in terms of percentage (%) and it is expressed as follows.

$$Investigation\ accuracy = \frac{(No.of\ cloud\ user - No.of\ malicous\ users)}{Total\ no.of\ cloud\ users} * 100 \quad ....Eqn\ (5.12)$$

Table 5.1: Tabulation For Investigation Accuracy

No. of cloud users	Investigation accuracy (%)			
	Secure provenance scheme	**Security as a Service Model**	**SecLaaS scheme**	**Proposed SFDC-SOMOPA**
10	58.74	62.65	66.58	82.27
20	60.68	64.55	68.59	84.24
30	62.36	66.65	70.58	86.16
40	64.85	68.69	72.25	88.14
50	66.12	70.85	74.69	90.26
60	68.74	72.08	76.36	92.31
70	70.85	74.98	78.65	94.31
80	72.86	76.36	80.25	95.73
90	74.27	78.06	82.95	96.15
100	76.78	80.96	84.25	97.06

The above table 5.1 demonstrates the investigation accuracy depending on the different number of cloud users.

The number of cloud user is varied from the range of 10 to 100 which is taken as input to carry out the experiments. In order to perform the simulation, the proposed SFDC-SOMOPA technique is compared with existing methods such as Secure Provenance Scheme by Jin Li et al., (2014), Security as a Service Model by Vijay Varadharajan and Udaya Tupakula (2014) and Secure-Logging-as-a-Service (SecLaaS) Scheme by Shams Zawoad et al., (2016).

From the table, it is observed that, four methods significantly improve the investigation accuracy with the respect to the number of cloud users.

But, comparatively the proposed SFDC-SOMOPA technique enhances the investigation accuracy than the other exiting methods. Based on the table value, the graph is plotted in below figure 5.5.

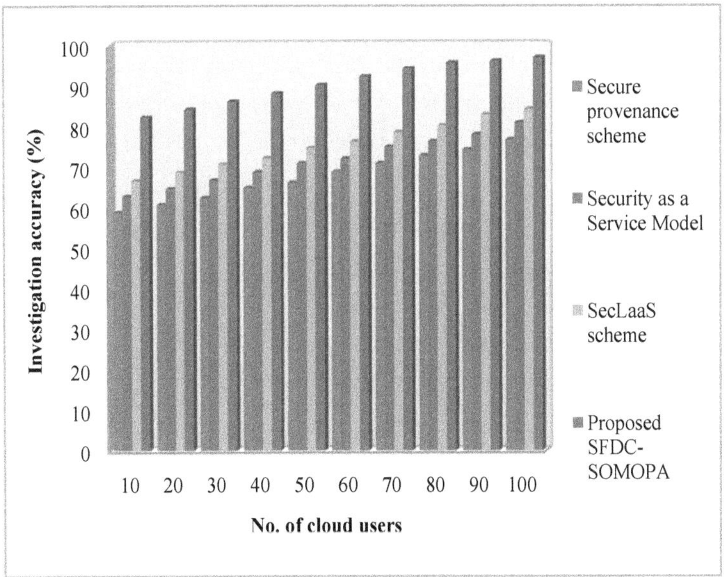

Figure 5.5: Measure of Investigation Accuracy

The figure 5.5 illustrates the measurement of investigation accuracy by using four methods such as proposed SFDC-SOMOPA technique, existing Secure Provenance Scheme, existing Security as a Service Model and existing Secure-Logging-as-a-Service (SecLaaS) Scheme.

The above figure clearly explains that the proposed SFDC-SOMOPA technique that achieves better improvement in the investigation accuracy as compared to other existing methods. This is due to, the proposed SFDC-SOMOPA technique performs the forensic investigation by collecting and isolating the evidence of malicious activities (cloud log files) with the help of Spatiotemporal Forensic Data Collector and watermarked forensic logging filter.

Besides, Swarm Optimized Multi-objective Proof Accumulator obtains the best global solution as evidence depending on the fitness function to detect the malicious user. This in turn follows investigation accuracy gets improved.

Moreover, the proposed SFDC-SOMOPA technique effectively improves the investigation accuracy up to 34% and 27% when compared with Secure Provenance Scheme by Jin Li et al., (2014) and Security as a Service Model by Vijay Varadharajan and Udaya Tupakula (2014) and 20% when compared with Secure-Logging-as-a-Service (SecLaaS) Scheme by Shams Zawoad et al., (2016).

5.7.2. Performance Analysis of Investigation Time

The Investigation time is measured as the amount of time consumed to collect the evidence from the cloud users. When the investigation time is less, then the technique is said to be more efficient. The Investigation time is measured in terms of milliseconds (ms) and it computed as follows.

$$Investigation\ time = No.of\ cloud\ users * time\ (to\ collect\ evidence) \quad ....\text{Eqn (5.13)}$$

Table 5.2: Tabulation For Investigation Time

No. of cloud users	**Investigation time (ms)**			
	Secure provenance scheme	**Security as a Service Model**	**SecLaaS scheme**	**Proposed SFDC-SOMOPA**
10	22.2	20.1	18.7	6.3
20	24.1	22.6	20.7	8.7
30	26.2	24.1	22.7	10.3
40	28.1	26.1	24.8	12.7
50	30.2	28.6	26.4	14.4
60	32.2	30.4	28.9	16.9
70	34.1	32.8	30.4	18.8
80	36.1	34.7	32.7	20.2
90	38.3	36.9	34.7	22.6
100	40.2	38.9	36.7	24.2

The above table 5.2 demonstrates the investigation time depending on different number of cloud users. The number of cloud user is varied from the range of 10 to 100 which is taken as input to carry out the experiments.

In order to perform the simulation, the proposed SFDC-SOMOPA technique is compared with existing methods such as Secure Provenance Scheme by Jin Li et al., (2014), Security as a Service Model by Vijay Varadharajan and Udaya Tupakula (2014) and Secure-Logging-as-a-Service (SecLaaS) Scheme by Shams Zawoad et al., (2016).

From the table, it is observed that, four methods considerably reduce the investigation time with respect to the number of cloud users. But, comparatively the proposed SFDC-SOMOPA technique reduces the investigation time than the other exiting methods. Based on the table value, the graph is plotted in below figure 5.6.

The figure 5.6 illustrates the measurement of investigation time by using four methods such as proposed SFDC-SOMOPA technique, existing Secure Provenance Scheme, existing Security as a Service Model and existing Secure-Logging-as-a-Service (SecLaaS) Scheme. The above figure clearly explains that the proposed SFDC-SOMOPA technique achieves better improvement on reducing the investigation time as compared to other existing methods.

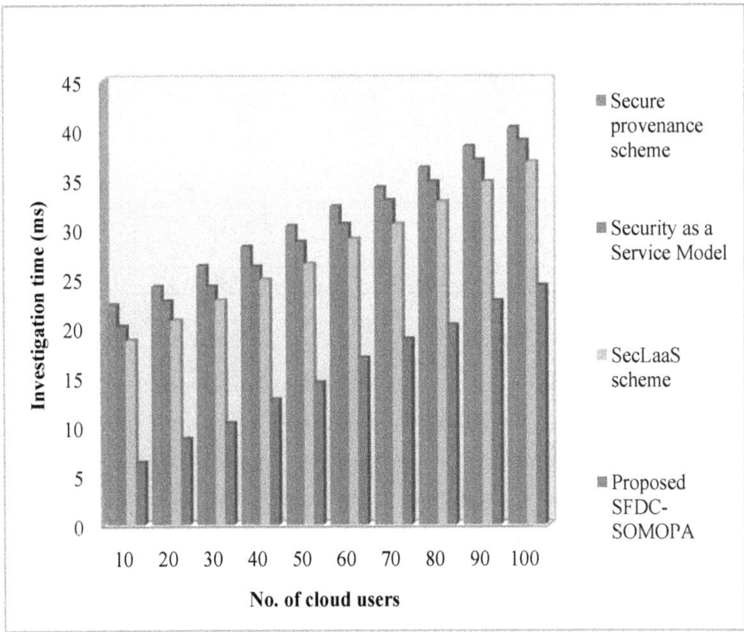

Figure 5.6: Measure of Investigation Time

In proposed SFDC-SOMOPA technique, the forensic investigation carry outs the fault tolerance Time Synchronization to allow the VMs for continuing the process without failure. This in turns, the investigation is performed with the minimal time.

Moreover, the proposed SFDC-SOMOPA technique effectively minimizes the investigation time by 52% and 49% when compared to Secure Provenance Scheme by Jin Li et al., (2014) and Security as a Service Model by Vijay Varadharajan and Udaya Tupakula (2014) and 46% when compared to Secure-Logging-as-a-Service (SecLaaS) Scheme by Shams Zawoad et al., (2016).

5.7.3. Performance Analysis of Filtering Efficiency

The Filtering efficiency is measured as the ratio of the number of cloud log files that are correctly separated to the total number of log files in virtual machines. When the filtering efficiency is high, then the technique is said to be more efficient. The Filtering efficiency is measured in terms of percentage (%) and it is evaluated as follow.

$$Filtering\ Efficiency = \frac{No.of\ isolated\ log\ files}{No.of\ cloud\ log\ files} * 100 \quad ....Eqn\ (5.14)$$

Table 5.3: Tabulation For Filtering Efficiency

No. of cloud log files	Filtering efficiency (%)			
	Secure provenance scheme	Security as a Service Model	SecLaaS scheme	Proposed SFDC-SOMOPA
5	52.85	57.06	67.87	79.36
10	54.85	59.36	69.79	81.72
15	56.41	61.25	72.97	83.77
20	58.63	63.74	74.68	85.79
25	60.85	65.98	76.49	87.94
30	62.35	67.06	78.69	89.89
35	64.24	69.36	80.49	91.58
40	66.12	72.25	82.87	93.58
45	68.25	73.74	84.79	95.79
50	70.74	76.98	86.97	97.79

The above table 5.3 demonstrates the filtering efficiency depends on the different number of cloud log files. The number of cloud log file is varied from the range of 5 to 50 which is taken as input to carry out the experiments. In order to perform the simulation, the proposed SFDC-SOMOPA technique is compared with existing methods such as Secure Provenance Scheme by Jin Li et al., (2014), Security as a Service Model by Vijay Varadharajan and Udaya Tupakula (2014) and Secure-Logging-as-a-Service (SecLaaS) Scheme by Shams Zawoad et al., (2016). From the table, it is observed that, four methods significantly improve the filtering efficiency with respect to the number of cloud log files.

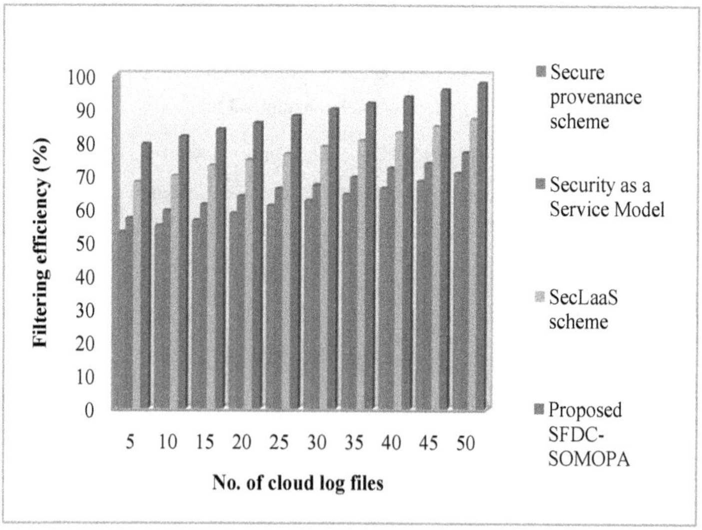

Figure 5.7: Measure of Filtering Efficiency

But, comparatively the proposed SFDC-SOMOPA technique enhances the filtering efficiency than the other exiting methods. Based on the table value, the graph is plotted in below figure 5.7.The figure 5.7 illustrates the measurement of filtering efficiency by employing four methods such as proposed SFDC-SOMOPA technique, existing Secure Provenance Scheme, existing Security as a Service Model and existing Secure-Logging-as-a-Service (SecLaaS) Scheme. The below figure clearly explains that, the proposed SFDC-SOMOPA technique achieves better enhancement on the filtering efficiency as compared to other existing methods.

The isolation of log files is carried out by using watermarked forensic logging filter in the proposed SFDC-SOMOPA technique. Through the spearman correlation measure, the normal or abnormal users are identified which ensures the data privacy of the malicious users and other cloud users. Then, the watermarking is used to mark the log files which are related with crimes. Thus, the exact malicious user is detected who initiates the crime event. Moreover, the proposed SFDC-SOMOPA technique effectively improves the filtering efficiency up to 45% and 33% when compared with Secure Provenance Scheme by Jin Li et al., (2014) and Security as a Service Model by Vijay Varadharajan and Udaya Tupakula (2014) and 15% when compared with Secure-Logging-as-a-Service (SecLaaS) Scheme by Shams Zawoad et al., (2016).

5.7.4. Performance Analysis of Processing Time

The Processing time is computed as the amount of time required to detect the malicious user from the cloud infrastructure. When the processing time is less, then the technique is said to be more efficient. The processing time is measured in terms of milliseconds (ms) and it is expressed as follows.

$$Processing\ time = No.of\ cloud\ users * Time\ (identify\ the\ malicious\ user) \quad \text{....Eqn (5.15)}$$

Table 5.4: Tabulation For Processing Time

No. of cloud users	**Processing time (ms)**			
	Secure provenance scheme	**Security as a Service Model**	**SecLaaS scheme**	**Proposed SFDC-SOMOPA**
10	40	38	26	16
20	42	40	29	18
30	44	42	32	20
40	46	44	35	22
50	48	46	38	24
60	50	48	42	26
70	52	50	46	28
80	54	52	49	30
90	56	54	52	32
100	58	56	55	34

The above table 5.4 demonstrates the processing time that depends on different number of cloud users. The number of cloud users is varied from the range of 10 to 100 which is taken as input to carry out the experiments. In order to perform the simulation, the proposed SFDC-SOMOPA technique is compared with existing methods such as Secure Provenance Scheme by Jin Li et al., (2014), Security as a Service Model by Vijay Varadharajan and Udaya Tupakula (2014) and Secure-Logging-as-a-Service (SecLaaS) Scheme by Shams Zawoad et al., (2016). From the table, it is observed that, four methods considerably reduce the processing time with respect to the number of cloud users. But, comparatively the proposed SFDC-SOMOPA technique minimizes the processing time than the other exiting methods. Based on the table value, the graph is plotted in below figure 5.8.

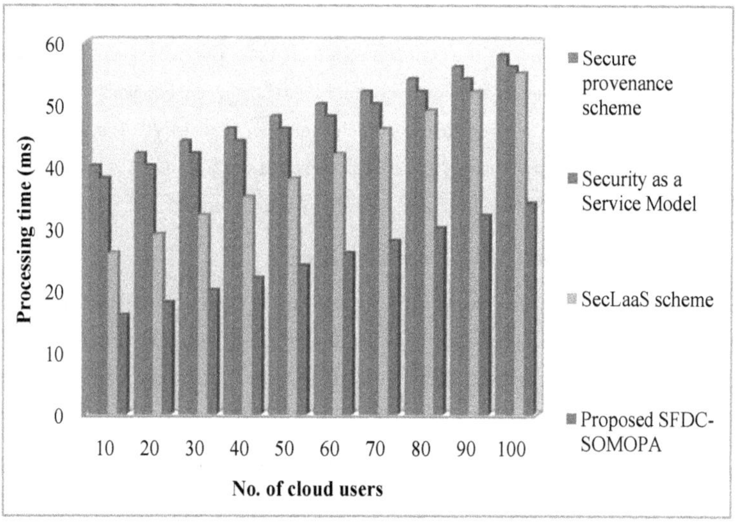

Figure 5.8: Measure of Processing Time

The figure 5.8 illustrates the measurement of processing time by using four methods such as proposed SFDC-SOMOPA technique, existing Secure Provenance Scheme, existing Security as a Service Model and existing Secure-Logging-as-a-Service (SecLaaS) Scheme. The above figure clearly explains that, the proposed SFDC-SOMOPA technique achieves better improvement on reducing the processing time as compared to other existing methods. This is due to, the proposed SFDC-SOMOPA technique applying the particle swarm optimization approach on the isolated cloud log files to detect optimal solution by authenticating the investigated evidence.

The particle which has the best fitness value is set as global best evidence based on the fitness function of multi objective functions which is done within minimal time. Moreover, the proposed SFDC-SOMOPA technique effectively reduces the processing time by 50% and 48% when compared to Secure Provenance Scheme by Jin Li et al., (2014) and Security as a Service Model by Vijay Varadharajan and Udaya Tupakula (2014) and 38% when compared to Secure-Logging-as-a-Service (SecLaaS) Scheme by Shams Zawoad et al., (2016).

5.7.5. Performance Analysis of Confidentiality Rate

The Confidentiality rate is defined as the ability of the system to protect the cloud user log files from the unauthorized access in cloud environment. When the confidentiality is high, then the technique is said to be more efficient. The Confidentiality rate is measured in terms of percentage (%) and it is computed as follows.

$$Confidentiality\ rate = \frac{No.of\ cloud\ log\ files\ are\ protected}{No.of\ cloud\ log\ files} * 100 \quad \text{....Eqn (5.16)}$$

Table 5.5: Tabulation For Confidentiality Rate

No. of cloud log files	Confidentiality rate (%)			
	Secure provenance scheme	Security as a Service Model	SecLaaS scheme	Proposed SFDC-SOMOPA
5	55.75	61.65	65.58	81.97
10	57.12	63.65	67.59	83.94
15	59.36	65.65	69.68	85.96
20	61.02	67.69	71.25	87.94
25	63.85	69.55	73.69	89.96
30	65.38	71.08	75.26	91.34
35	67.25	73.98	77.65	93.56
40	69.32	75.26	79.35	95.54
45	71.25	77.06	81.55	96.15
50	73.78	79.96	83.25	97.52

The above table 5.5 demonstrates the confidentiality rate depending on different number of cloud log files. The number of cloud log file is varied from the range of 5 to 50 which is taken as input to carry out the experiments. In order to perform the simulation, the proposed SFDC-SOMOPA technique is compared with existing methods such as Secure provenance scheme by Jin Li et al., (2014), Security as a Service Model by Vijay Varadharajan and Udaya Tupakula (2014) and Secure-Logging-as-a-Service (SecLaaS) Scheme by Shams Zawoad et al., (2016).

From the table, it is observed that, four methods significantly enhance the confidentiality rate with respect to the number of cloud log files. But, comparatively the proposed SFDC-SOMOPA technique improves the confidentiality rate than the other exiting methods. Based on the table value, the graph is plotted in below figure 5.9.

The figure 5.9 illustrates the measurement of confidentiality rate by using four methods such as proposed SFDC-SOMOPA technique, existing Secure Provenance Scheme, existing Security as a Service Model and existing Secure-Logging-as-a-Service (SecLaaS) Scheme. The above figure clearly explains that, the proposed SFDC-SOMOPA technique achieves better improvement on the confidentiality rate as compared to other existing methods.

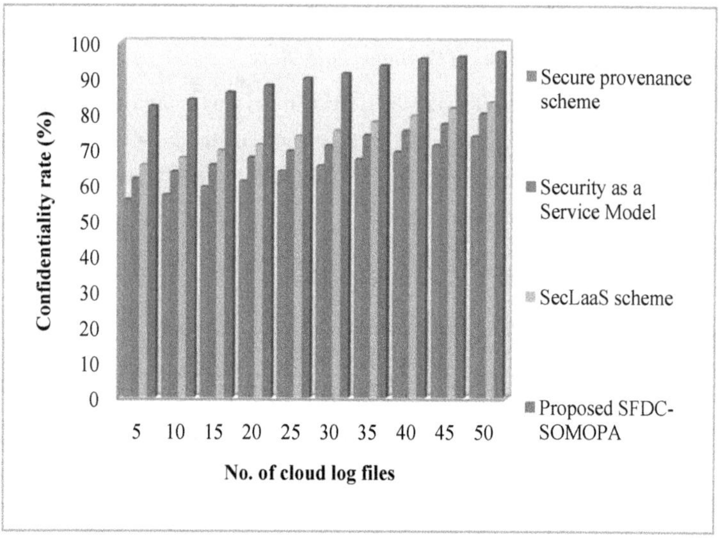

Figure 5.9: Measure of Confidentiality Rate

The proposed SFDC-SOMOPA technique prevents the multiple cloud users of log files from unauthorized modifications while submitting the evidence to the proof accumulator. By validating the investigated log filter, the Swarm optimization technique determines the malicious user with admissible evidence which ensures the privacy level of the cloud user log files to guarantee the confidentiality. Moreover, the proposed SFDC-SOMOPA technique effectively improves the confidentiality rate up to 41% and 28% when compared with Secure Provenance Scheme by Jin Li et al., (2014) and Security as a Service Model by Vijay Varadharajan and Udaya Tupakula (2014) and 22% when compared with Secure-Logging-as-a-Service (SecLaaS) Scheme by Shams Zawoad et al., (2016).

5.8. Summary

The Spatiotemporal Forensic Data Collector and Swarm Optimized Multi-Objective Proof Accumulator (SFDC-SOMOPA) technique is implemented to find out the malicious user who initiates the crime on the cloud environment. The proposed SFDC-SOMOPA technique provides cloud services in secured manner by performing three processes such as collecting the cloud log files from different sources, isolating cloud log files and reporting the acceptable evidence of malicious activities. Initially, in the proposed SFDC-SOMOPA technique various cloud log files are effectively collected from different resources with the application of Spatiotemporal Data Collector, fault tolerance and Time Synchronization. Thereby, accuracy in the investigation of evidence of malicious activities is improved with minimized time. Secondly, the multiple cloud log files are isolated from the collected cloud log files by introducing the Watershed forensic logging filter (WFLF) in the proposed SFDC-SOMOPA technique. Thus, the filtering efficiency gets improved to ensure the data privacy of the malicious users and other cloud users.

Finally, by using Swarm Optimized Multi-objective Proof Accumulator, the multi-objective functions as the evidence of malicious activities are reported to the proof accumulator which guarantees the confidentiality. Then, the submitted evidences of cloud log files are optimized by validating the investigated log filter with the help of particle swarm optimization. Through the particle swarm optimization, the malicious user is detected with minimized processing time by identifying the global best evidence depending on the fitness function. Furthermore, the performance of proposed SFDC-SOMOPA technique is tested with the following metrics such as investigation accuracy, investigation time, filtering efficiency, processing time and confidentiality rate. From the experiments results, it is clear that, the proposed SFDC-SOMOPA technique performs secured cloud services through the cloud forensic investigation with the improvement of investigation accuracy, filtering efficiency and confidentiality rate up to 27%, 31% and 30% when compared to the state-of-the-art works. In addition, the proposed SFDC-SOMOPA technique reduces the investigation time and processing time by 49% and 45% when compared to the state-of-the-art works.

Chapter VI

Performance Of Cloud Forensic Analysis For Secured File Transmission In Government Sectors

6.1. Introduction

Cloud computing is an internet based computing system that provides different services to the cloud users in easiest manner for performing various cloud applications. Cloud computing is employed to link the huge number of systems in private or public networks which ensure extensible infrastructure for application, data and file storage.

The cloud computing is an essential model for outsourcing the data because it reduces the cost for computation, application hosting, content storage and delivery. In cloud environment, the security to the cloud data and privacy of user are the major concern because of the presence of malicious users.

In order to find out the malicious user in cloud platform, cloud forensic as digital forensic procedure is introduced in crime investigation. The cloud forensic investigation is carried out with log files of multiple cloud users in the four phases as collection, observation, analysis and report on cloud environment.

Though different research works are employed to trace the malicious users on cloud, the confidentiality and privacy throughout the investigation remained unaddressed. Previous chapters are concentrated on performing the forensic investigation to detect the exact malicious user with acceptable evidences that causes crime incident on cloud by reporting the evidence of malicious activities.

In this research, the three proposed techniques such as Spatio-Temporal Forensic Data Collector and Logging filter (STFDC-LF), Gene Optimized Multi-objective Proof Accumulator (GOMOPA) and Spatiotemporal Forensic Data Collector and Swarm Optimized Multi-objective Proof Accumulator (SFDC-SOMOPA) techniques are implemented with the aim of achieving secured cloud services with better confidentiality over a cloud environment. These proposed techniques are utilized for cloud forensic analysis to carry out confidential file transfer on government sectors.

In cloud platform, large number of end users i.e. employees, managers, administrators and supervisors are deployed across multiple departments for specific government sector.

In the government sectors, the information assurance is essential one to ensure that the content of file is not altered or interrupted by unwanted parties while transferring the files that guarantees the data confidentiality. In addition, there is necessity to protect the identity and location of cloud user on government sector from malicious user which improves the privacy level of user. From that, the privacy, confidentiality and security are achieved by preventing the statistical analysis of the cloud data from malicious user modification.

In cloud computing, cloud forensic analysis is carried out to find the malicious user by performing the investigation on a network. The forensic investigation is performed by collecting, isolating and reporting the evidence of malicious user to court of law for discovering the malicious user on cloud. Let us consider a number of users in particular government sector unit to outsource their confidential files such as DOC, XLS, JPG, PDF, ZIP, etc... over a cloud environment.

Then, the cloud server ensures unique user id and password for each user of specific sector unit. Through the Cloud Service Provider (CSP), the respective files from cloud server are extracted by specific user using that issued particular user id and password. From that, the files on cloud server is only accessed by authorized users who having the specific user id and password.

In case, malicious user hack the data on cloud while transferring the files between authorized user and cloud server which leads to confidential data loss. At this point, there is chance to make modifications on cloud data by unauthorized user for the particular sector unit. Thereby, confidentiality and privacy level of data get reduced.

Therefore, the proposed research is utilized to detect the malicious user who causes crime incident by providing admissible evidence with the application of proposed STFDC-LF technique, GOMOPA technique and SFDC-SOMOPA technique on the cloud environment. The figure 6.1 illustrates the architecture diagram of cloud forensic analysis for secured cloud services.

As shown in figure 6.1, the secured file transmission in government sectors is achieved through the proposed techniques as STFDC-LF, GOMOPA and SFDC-SOMOPA by identifying the malicious user in cloud environment. Generally, the confidential file transmission is performed between cloud users and server in a particular government sector over a cloud. If the files are attacked or altered by unauthorized parties, the security for the confidential data gets affected. At that time, the following processes are carried out to identify the malicious user.

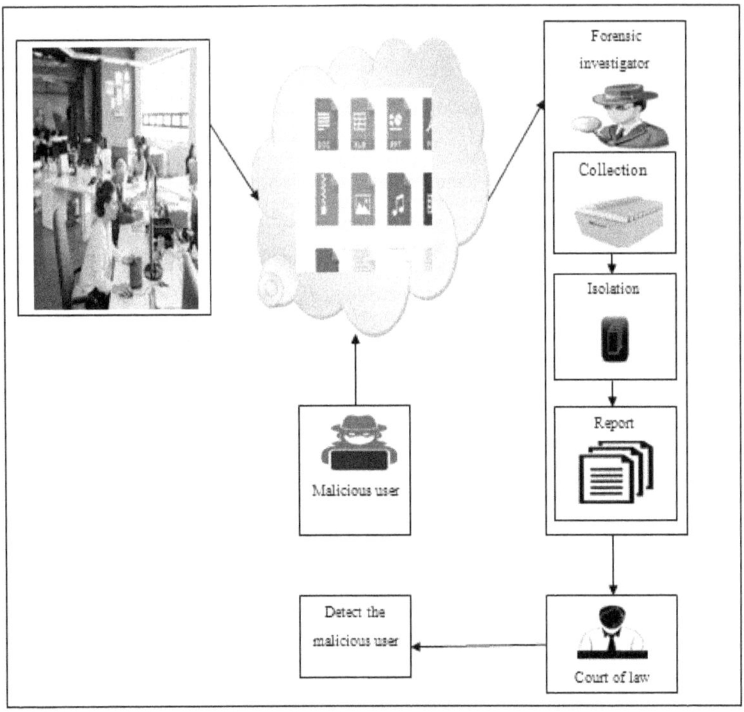

Figure 6.1: Cloud Forensic Analysis For Secured Cloud Services

At first, the proposed Spatio-temporal Forensic Data Collector and Logging filter (STFDC-LF) technique performs the forensic investigation with Spatio-temporal Forensic Data Collector by collecting the cloud log files of multiple cloud users from various sources such as application logs, storage logs, computing logs and network logs. Then, the Event Activity Time Synchronization is carried out to handle the multiple cloud files at a specific time. Followed by, the evidences of malicious activities are filtered i.e. isolated which are relevant to the crime event with the help of Forensic Logging Filter. From that, the evidences of the malicious activities are extracted from cloud server by the investigator in order to identify malicious user who initiates crime incident.

After that, the proposed Gene Optimized Multi-objective Proof Accumulator (GOMOPA) technique is carried out with the discovered evidences of the malicious activities by STFDC-LF technique.

Then, the filtered evidences are submitted to the proof accumulator based on the multi-objective functions by the forensic investigator. The multi-objective functions contains the information such as evidence of the malicious activity, proof of integrity, provenance information, proof of data possession, time stamp information and location information. Finally, the multi-objective functions are optimized with the help of gene based approach by extracting the exact evidence to identify malicous user who causes for the particular crime incident. The extracted evidence of malicious activities are required to be accepted by the court proceedings. From that, through the GOMOPA technique, the malicious user is discovered by submitting the admissible evidences. Besides, the proposed Spatiotemporal Forensic Data Collector and Swarm Optimized Multi-Objective Proof Accumulator (SFDC-SOMOPA) technique is introduced for cloud forensic analysis in order to perform the privacy preserved investigation. Initially, the Spatiotemporal Forensic Data Collector is used to acquire the multiple users of cloud log files related with physical location and the temporal information.

Then, the Fault tolerant Time Synchronization method is engaged to extort the precise time for the evidence of malicious activities. After that, Watershed Forensic Logging Filter (WFLF) is introduced to perform isolation process for extracting the specific types of log information and reorganizing them by time, IP address and User ID. The Watermarked forensic logging filter analysis the unique user ID and specific event of the temporally retrieved log files to isolate the cloud log files of multiple users who shares the same infrastructure. Then, the log files are separated as relevant or irrelevant to the event happed on cloud. Thus, privacy of normal users are preserved from the malicious users. Finally, Swarm Optimized Multi-objective Proof Accumulator (SOMOPA) is used for reporting the multi objective function to the proof accumulator in order to extract malicious user who launches the crime depending on the fitness calculation. Moreover, the exact malicious user is identified with acceptable evidence by discovering the IP address of malicious user with the application of three proposed techniques. By the identification of malicious user, the confidential files on government sector unit being transmitted in a secured manner.

In order to evaluate the performance, the proposed Spatio-Temporal Forensic Data Collector and Logging filter (STFDC-LF), Gene Optimized Multi-objective Proof Accumulator (GOMOPA) and Spatiotemporal Forensic Data Collector and Swarm Optimized Multi-objective Proof Accumulator (SFDC-SOMOPA) technique are evaluated by using java language with CloudSim network simulator. In cloud environment, CloudSim simulator provides different services with the accessible resources and a particular toolkit is considered as simulation platform.

With the help of CloudSim simulator, the malicious user is identified with minimal time by performing the forensic investigation. The number of cloud user is taken as 10 to 100 and the number of cloud log files is considered as 5 to 50 to carry out the experiments. The proposed STFDC-LF technique and GOMOPA technique are implemented by CloudSim simulator using Amazon EC2 dataset.

In addition, the proposed SFDC-SOMOPA technique carry out the experiments by CloudSim simulator using Amazon access sample dataset. The Amazon access sample dataset is obtained from the UCI repository. The Amazon access sample dataset comprises of four types of attributes such as Person_Attribute, Resource_ID, Group_ID and System_Support_ID.

6.2. Performance Analysis For Proposed STFDC-LF, GOMOPA AND SFDC-SOMOPA Techniques

The performance of proposed Spatio-Temporal Forensic Data Collector and Logging filter (STFDC-LF), Gene Optimized Multi-objective Proof Accumulator (GOMOPA) and Spatiotemporal Forensic Data Collector and Swarm Optimized Multi-objective Proof Accumulator (SFDC-SOMOPA) techniques are implemented by java language with CloudSim network simulator.

In order to conduct the experiments, the proposed STFDC-LF technique and GOMOPA technique and SFDC-SOMOPA technique are compared with the existing methods such as Secure-Logging-as-a-Service (SecLaaS) Scheme by Shams Zawoad et al., (2016), Forensic Open-Stack Tools (FROST) by Josiah Dykstra and Alan T. Sherman (2013) and Security as a Service Model by Vijay Varadharajan and Udaya Tupakula (2014).

The performance of proposed techniques is evaluated with the help of parameters such as investigation accuracy, investigation time, filtering efficiency, confidentiality rate and processing time. The detailed result analyses of these metrics are elaborated in further section.

6.2.1. *Performance Analysis of Investigation Accuracy*

The Investigation accuracy is referred as the ratio of the number of malicious users that is correctly identified to the total number of cloud users in cloud environment. The mathematical formula for investigation accuracy is measured as follows.

$$Investigation\ accuracy = \frac{(No.of\ user - No.of\ malicous\ users)}{Totol\ no.of\ cloud\ users} * 100 \quad \text{....Eqn (6.1)}$$

The investigation accuracy is measured in terms of percentage (%). Higher value of investigation accuracy ensures better performance of the technique.

Table 6.1: Tabulation For Investigation Accuracy

No. of cloud users	Investigation accuracy (%)											
	Amazon EC2 dataset						Amazon access sample dataset					
	SecLaaS scheme	FROST	Security as a Service Model	Proposed STFDC-LF	Proposed GOMOPA	Proposed SFDC-SOMOPA	SecLaaS scheme	FROST	Security as a Service Model	Proposed STFDC-LF	Proposed GOMOPA	Proposed SFDC-SOMOPA
10	64.89	56.36	60.46	68.87	70.06	72.06	66.58	58.99	62.65	76.15	80.36	82.27
20	66.98	58.72	62.79	70.79	72.69	74.69	68.59	60.98	64.55	78.28	82.16	84.24
30	68.89	60.36	64.46	72.87	74.06	76.06	70.58	62.89	66.65	80.19	84.26	86.16
40	70.06	62.79	66.98	74.68	76.06	78.69	72.25	64.99	68.69	82.29	86.28	88.14
50	72.69	64.46	68.89	76.49	78.69	80.49	74.69	66.88	70.85	84.69	88.15	90.26
60	74.06	66.98	70.06	78.69	80.49	82.87	76.36	68.95	72.08	86.12	90.05	92.31
70	76.06	68.89	72.69	80.49	82.87	84.79	78.65	70.99	74.98	88.96	91.26	94.31
80	78.69	70.06	74.06	82.87	84.79	86.97	80.25	72.99	76.36	90.17	92.15	95.73
90	80.49	72.69	76.06	84.79	86.97	88.96	82.95	74.98	78.06	92.26	94.06	96.15
100	82.87	74.06	78.69	86.97	88.96	90.96	84.25	76.98	80.96	94.32	95.14	97.06

The above table 6.1 illustrates the comparative result analysis of investigation accuracy using proposed STFDC-LF technique and GOMOPA technique and SFDC-SOMOPA technique with the existing methods such as Secure-Logging-as-a-Service (SecLaaS) Scheme by Shams Zawoad et al., (2016), Forensic Open-Stack Tools (FROST) by Josiah Dykstra and Alan T. Sherman (2013) and Security as a Service Model by Vijay Varadharajan and Udaya Tupakula (2014). The number of cloud users is considered from 10 to 100 which are taken as input to perform the simulation.

As shown in above table, the performance analysis of investigation accuracy in the proposed techniques and existing methods has shown a significant improvement with respect to the different number of cloud users. However, the proposed SFDC-SOMOPA technique ensures better results in the improvement of investigation accuracy than other methods. The graph is plotted in below figure 6.2 by utilizing table values from the table 6.1.

The figure 6.2 shows the measurement of investigation accuracy by comparing the three proposed techniques as STFDC-LF technique and GOMOPA technique and SFDC-SOMOPA technique with existing methods such as Secure-Logging-as-a-Service (SecLaaS) Scheme, Forensic Open-Stack Tools (FROST) and Security as a Service Model. The above figure clearly describes that the proposed SFDC-SOMOPA technique effectively enhances the investigation accuracy than the other proposed and exiting methods while using the Amazon access sample dataset.

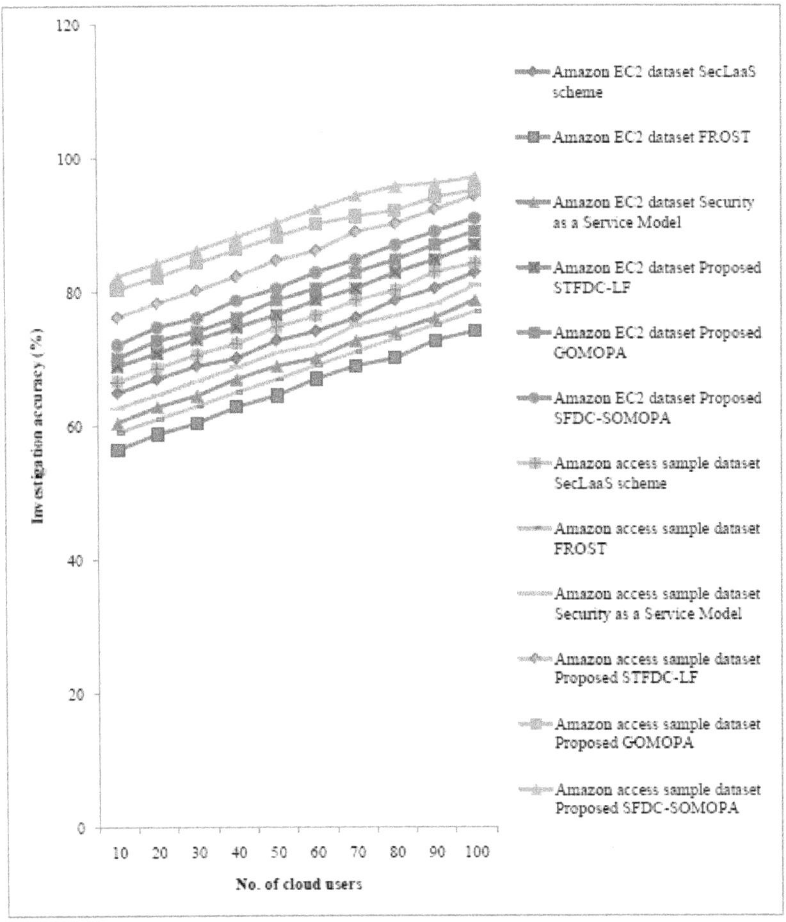

Figure 6.2: Measure of Investigation Accuracy

Thus the effective forensic investigation on specific government sector unit is carried out to detect the exact malicious user who initiates crime actions by using proposed SFDC-SOMOPA technique.

At first, the proposed SFDC-SOMOPA technique efficiently acquires the cloud log files of multiple cloud users to sector unit from different resources by using the Spatiotemporal Forensic Data Collector.

Here, Fault tolerant time synchronization is carried out to collect the evidences with exact time.

Then, these collected log files (evidences) of malicious activities are isolated which are relevant or irrelevant with crime event by watermarked forensic logging filter. Then, Swarm Optimized Multi-objective Proof Accumulator extracts the exact evidence of malicious user depends on the multi-objective functions.

With the help of evidence of malicious user, the location (IP address) of that user and exact time of crime action are extracted.

Moreover, during the forensic investigation, the proposed SFDC-SOMOPA technique uses Amazon access sample dataset for improving the investigation accuracy to detect the exact malicious user from normal users by 20% and 34% when compared to Secure-Logging-as-a-Service (SecLaaS) Scheme by Shams Zawoad et al., (2016), Forensic Open-Stack Tools (FROST) by Josiah Dykstra and Alan T. Sherman (2013) and 27% when compared to Security as a Service Model by Vijay Varadharajan and Udaya Tupakula (2014).

6.2.2. Performance Analysis of Investigation Time

The investigation time is measured as the amount of time consumed by the cloud forensic investigator to collect the evidences from the cloud users. The mathematical formula for investigation time is measured as.

$$Investigation\ Time = N * time\ (to\ collect\ evidence) \quad ....\text{Eqn } (6.2)$$

The investigation time is measured in terms of milliseconds (ms). If the investigation time is less, then the technique said to be more efficient.

Table 6.2: Tabulation For Investigation Time

No. of cloud users	Investigation time (ms)											
	Amazon EC2 dataset						Amazon access sample dataset					
	SecLaaS scheme	FROST	Security as a Service Model	Proposed STFDC-LF	Proposed GOMOPA	Proposed SFDC-SOMOPA	SecLaaS scheme	FROST	Security as a Service Model	Proposed STFDC-LF	Proposed GOMOPA	Proposed SFDC-SOMOPA
10	26.1	32.2	30.3	16.8	12.5	8.9	18.7	22.1	20.1	14.8	10.4	6.3
20	28.2	34.2	32.6	18.9	14.5	10.9	20.7	24.6	22.6	16.9	12.7	8.7
30	30.1	36.1	34.2	20.5	16.6	12.8	22.7	26.1	24.1	18.8	14.4	10.3
40	32.2	38.1	36.8	22.5	18.9	14.9	24.8	28.6	26.1	20.1	16.9	12.7
50	34.6	40.2	38.1	24.9	20.8	16.8	26.4	30.4	28.6	22.6	18.7	14.4
60	36.1	42.1	40.1	26.6	22.8	18.9	28.9	32.8	30.4	24.1	20.1	16.9
70	38.9	44.1	42.6	28.6	24.5	20.9	30.4	34.7	32.8	26.1	22.6	18.8
80	40.1	46.3	44.1	30.5	26.6	22.9	32.7	36.9	34.7	28.6	24.1	20.2
90	42.2	48.1	46.1	32.5	28.2	24.9	34.7	38.9	36.9	30.4	26.1	22.6
100	44.3	49.6	48.1	34.2	30.9	27.9	36.7	40.9	38.9	32.8	28.6	24.2

The above table 6.2 illustrates the comparative result analysis of investigation time using proposed STFDC-LF technique and GOMOPA technique and SFDC-SOMOPA technique with the existing methods such as Secure-Logging-as-a-Service (SecLaaS) Scheme by Shams Zawoad et al., (2016), Forensic Open-Stack Tools (FROST) by Josiah Dykstra and Alan T. Sherman (2013) and Security as a Service Model by Vijay Varadharajan and Udaya Tupakula (2014). The number of cloud users is considered from 10 to 100 which are taken as input to perform the simulation. As shown in above table, the performance of analysis of investigation time in the proposed methods and existing methods is significantly reduced with respect to the number of cloud users. However, the proposed SFDC-SOMOPA technique ensures better results on reducing the investigation time than the other methods. The graph is plotted in below figure 6.3 by utilizing the table values from the table 6.2.

The figure 6.3 shows the measurement of investigation time by comparing the three proposed techniques as STFDC-LF technique and GOMOPA technique and SFDC-SOMOPA technique with existing methods such as Secure-Logging-as-a-Service (SecLaaS) Scheme, Forensic Open-Stack Tools (FROST) and Security as a Service Model. The below figure clearly describes that the proposed SFDC-SOMOPA technique effectively reduces the investigation time than the other proposed and existing methods.

Thus, forensic investigator collects the cloud log files of various resources related with physical location and the temporal information by using Spatiotemporal Forensic Data Collector in the proposed SFDC-SOMOPA technique.

Here, the Fault tolerant time synchronization allows the VMs for continuing the process without failure. From that, the investigator acquires the evidences of malicious user with minimal amount of time who initiates crime action while transferring confidential files between authorized user and server on cloud. Moreover, with the help of Amazon access sample dataset ,the proposed SFDC-SOMOPA technique minimizes the investigation time to collect the evidence of malicious activities by 46% and 53% when compared to Secure-Logging-as-a-Service (SecLaaS) Scheme by Shams Zawoad et al., (2016),

Forensic Open-Stack Tools (FROST) by Josiah Dykstra and Alan T. Sherman (2013) and 49% when compared to Security as a Service Model by Vijay Varadharajan and Udaya Tupakula (2014).

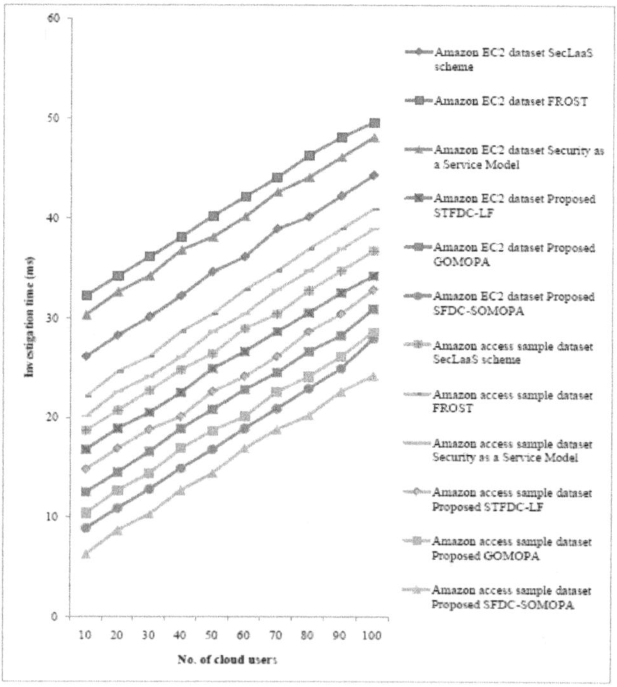

Figure 6.3: Measure of Investigation Time

6.2.3. *Performance Analysis of Filtering Efficiency*

The filtering efficiency is defined as the ratio of the number of cloud log files which is correctly isolated from collected cloud log files that is related or unrelated to crime activities to the total number of log files in virtual machines. The mathematical formula for filtering efficiency is described as given below.

$$FE = \frac{No.of\ isolated\ cloud\ \ log\ files}{Total\ no.of\ collected\ cloud\ log\ files} * 100 \ \text{....Eqn (6.3)}$$

The filtering efficiency is measured in terms of percentage (%). The higher value of filtering efficiency provides better performance of the technique.

The above table 6.3 illustrates the comparative result analysis of filtering efficiency using proposed STFDC-LF technique and GOMOPA technique and SFDC-SOMOPA technique with the existing methods such as Secure-Logging-as-a-Service (SecLaaS) Scheme by Shams Zawoad et al., (2016), Forensic Open-Stack Tools (FROST) by Josiah Dykstra and Alan T. Sherman (2013) and Security as a Service Model by Vijay Varadharajan and Udaya Tupakula (2014). The number of cloud log file is considered from 5 to 50 which are taken as input to perform the simulation.

Table 6.3: Tabulation For Filtering Efficiency

No. of cloud log files	Filtering efficiency (%)											
	Amazon EC2 dataset						Amazon access sample dataset					
	SecLaaS scheme	FROST	Security as a Service Model	Proposed STFDC-LF	Proposed GOMOPA	Proposed SFDC-SOMOPA	SecLaaS scheme	FROST	Security as a Service Model	Proposed STFDC-LF	Proposed GOMOPA	Proposed SFDC-SOMOPA
5	50.28	38.96	45.58	55.58	59.65	65.56	67.87	53.06	57.06	73.89	77.46	79.36
10	53.06	40.56	46.95	57.59	61.55	66.93	69.79	55.69	59.36	75.98	79.79	81.72
15	55.69	43.23	48.69	59.68	63.28	68.56	72.97	57.64	61.25	77.46	81.79	83.77
20	57.64	45.28	50.93	61.25	65.69	70.85	74.68	59.84	63.74	79.79	83.49	85.79
25	59.84	47.25	52.65	63.69	67.85	73.78	76.49	61.32	65.98	81.79	85.85	87.94
30	61.32	48.05	54.56	65.36	69.08	75.55	78.69	63.25	67.06	83.49	87.49	89.89
35	63.25	50.96	56.96	67.65	71.98	77.85	80.49	65.96	69.36	86.49	89.85	91.58
40	65.96	53.75	58.25	69.25	73.36	79.85	82.87	67.25	72.25	88.79	91.85	93.58
45	67.25	55.96	60.85	71.95	75.06	82.85	84.79	69.96	73.74	90.49	93.85	95.79
50	69.96	57.74	62.36	74.25	77.96	84.85	86.97	72.96	76.98	92.49	95.85	97.79

As shown in above table, the performance of analysis of filtering efficiency in the proposed methods and existing methods is significantly improved with respect to the number of cloud log files.

However, the proposed SFDC-SOMOPA technique ensures better results in the improvement of filtering efficiency than the other methods. The graph is plotted in below figure 6.4 by utilizing the table values from the table 6.3.

The figure 6.4 shows the measurement of filtering efficiency by comparing the three proposed techniques as STFDC-LF technique and GOMOPA technique and SFDC-SOMOPA technique with existing methods such as Secure-Logging-as-a-Service (SecLaaS) Scheme, Forensic Open-Stack Tools (FROST) and Security as a Service Model.

The above figure clearly describes that the proposed SFDC-SOMOPA technique effectively enhances the filtering efficiency than the other proposed and exiting methods.

Thus, the proposed SFDC-SOMOPA technique introduces watermarked forensic logging filter to separate the evidences of malicious activities i.e. cloud log files from the collected log files which are relevant or irrelevant to the crime action performed on cloud.

Here, the spearman correlation measure is carried out to isolate the malicious users of log files from normal users of log files thereby the data privacy for both malicious users and other cloud users is preserved.

Then, the proposed SFDC-SOMOPA technique assigns mark to the relevant log files of malicious activities.

From that, the accurate evidences of malicious activities are extracted by performing filtering process.

Moreover, the proposed SFDC-SOMOPA technique improves the filtering efficiency by using Amazon access sample dataset up to 15% and 42% when compared to Secure-Logging-as-a-Service (SecLaaS) Scheme by Shams Zawoad et al., (2016), Forensic Open-Stack Tools (FROST) by Josiah Dykstra and Alan T. Sherman (2013) and 33% when compared to Security as a Service Model by Vijay Varadharajan and Udaya Tupakula (2014).

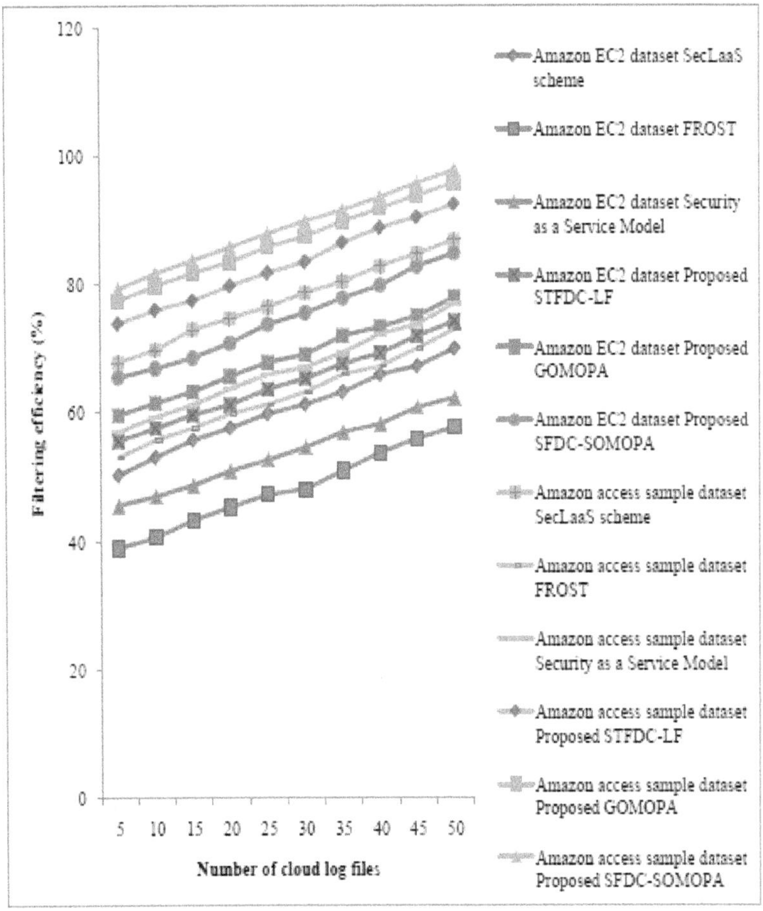

Figure 6.4: Measure of Filtering Efficiency

6.2.4. Performance Analysis of Confidentiality Rate

The confidentiality is the ability of the system to protect the cloud user log files from unauthorized access in cloud environment. The mathematical formula for confidentiality rate is measured as follows.

$$Confidentiality\,rate = \frac{Number\ \ of\ \ log\ files\ are\ protected}{Total\ \ number\ \ of\ cloud\ \log\ files} * 100 \quad \text{....Eqn (6.4)}$$

The confidentiality rate is measured in terms of percentage (%). If the confidentiality rate is high, then the technique is said to be more efficient.

Table 6.4: Tabulation For Confidentiality Rate

No. of cloud log files	Confidentiality rate (%)											
	Amazon EC2 dataset						Amazon access sample dataset					
	SecLaaS scheme	FROST	Security as a Service Model	Proposed STFDC-LF	Proposed GOMOPA	Proposed SFDC-SOMOPA	SecLaaS scheme	FROST	Security as a Service Model	Proposed STFDC-LF	Proposed GOMOPA	Proposed SFDC-SOMOPA
5	63.89	55.36	59.46	67.87	69.06	71.06	65.58	57.99	61.65	75.55	79.56	81.97
10	65.95	57.72	61.79	69.79	71.69	73.69	67.59	59.88	63.65	77.28	81.66	83.94
15	67.89	59.86	63.46	71.87	73.06	75.86	69.68	61.69	65.65	79.99	83.66	85.96
20	69.56	61.79	65.98	73.58	75.06	77.49	71.25	63.99	67.69	81.69	85.58	87.94
25	71.69	63.46	67.89	75.49	77.69	79.49	73.69	65.88	69.55	83.69	87.95	89.96
30	73.06	65.98	69.06	77.39	79.49	81.57	75.26	67.95	71.08	85.22	89.95	91.34
35	75.06	67.99	71.69	79.49	81.87	83.79	77.65	69.99	73.98	87.96	90.36	93.56
40	77.49	69.06	73.06	81.87	83.79	85.67	79.35	71.99	75.26	89.87	92.25	95.54
45	79.69	71.69	75.06	83.79	85.97	87.96	81.55	73.98	77.06	91.96	93.66	96.15
50	81.87	73.06	77.69	85.97	87.96	89.96	83.25	75.98	79.96	93.62	96.64	97.52

The above table 6.4 illustrates the comparative result analysis of confidentiality rate using proposed STFDC-LF technique and GOMOPA technique and SFDC-SOMOPA technique with the existing methods such as Secure-Logging-as-a-Service (SecLaaS) Scheme by Shams Zawoad et al., (2016), Forensic Open-Stack Tools (FROST) by Josiah Dykstra and Alan T. Sherman (2013) and Security as a Service Model by Vijay Varadharajan and Udaya Tupakula (2014). The number of cloud log file is considered from 5 to 50 which are taken as input to perform the simulation.As shown in above table, the performance analysis of confidentiality rate in the proposed techniques and existing methods has shown improvement with respect to the number of cloud log files. However, the proposed SFDC-SOMOPA technique ensures better results in the improvement of confidentiality rate than the other methods. The graph is plotted in below figure 6.5 by utilizing the table values from the table 6.4.The figure 6.5 shows the measurement of confidentiality rate by comparing the three proposed techniques as STFDC-LF technique and GOMOPA technique and SFDC-SOMOPA technique with existing methods such as Secure-Logging-as-a-Service (SecLaaS) Scheme, Forensic Open-Stack Tools (FROST) and Security as a Service Model. The below figure clearly describes that the proposed SFDC-SOMOPA technique effectively enhances the confidentiality rate than the other proposed and exiting methods.Thus, the proposed SFDC-SOMOPA technique effectively optimizes the multi-objective functions of evidences in the multi-objective proof accumulator. The multi-objective functions are contained with malicious cloud user activities, proof of integrity, provenance information, proof of data possession, time stamp and location information. These objective functions are reported to the accumulator by investigator which avoids the unauthorized access of log files from server. Then, the Swarm optimization technique is used to trace the exact malicious user with acceptable evidences from the watermarked forensic logging filter by authenticating the investigated evidences.

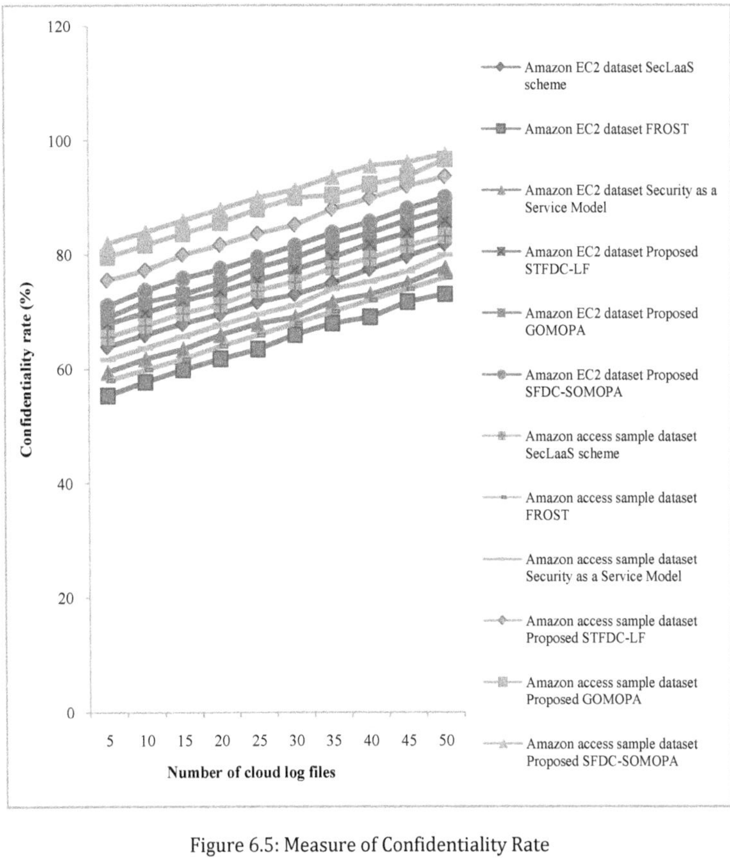

Figure 6.5: Measure of Confidentiality Rate

Thus, it is clearly describes that the privacy level of the cloud user log files are persevered which guarantees the confidentiality rate. Moreover, the proposed SFDC-SOMOPA technique improves the confidentiality rate up to 22% and 35% when compared to Secure-Logging-as-a-Service (SecLaaS) Scheme by Shams Zawoad et al., (2016), Forensic Open-Stack Tools (FROST) by Josiah Dykstra and Alan T. Sherman (2013) and 28% when compared to Security as a Service Model by Vijay Varadharajan and Udaya Tupakula (2014).

6.2.5. Performance Analysis of Processing Time

Based on the reports of admissible evidences, the processing time is measured as the amount of time that is consumed to identify the malicious user on cloud. The mathematical formula for processing time is measured as follows.

$Processing\ Time = Number\ of\ cloud\ users * Time\ (identify\ the\ malicious\ user)$ ....Eqn (6.5)

The processing time is measured in terms of milliseconds (ms). If the processing time is less, then the technique is said to be more efficient.

Table 6.5: Tabulation For Processing Time

No. of cloud users	Processing time (ms)											
	Amazon EC2 dataset						Amazon access sample dataset					
	SecLaaS scheme	FROST	Security as a Service Model	Proposed STFDC-LF	Proposed GOMOPA	Proposed SFDC-SOMOPA	SecLaaS scheme	FROST	Security as a Service Model	Proposed STFDC-LF	Proposed GOMOPA	Proposed SFDC-SOMOPA
10	36	42	40	26	22	18	28	32	30	24	20	16
20	38	44	42	28	24	20	30	34	32	26	22	18
30	40	46	44	30	26	22	32	36	34	28	24	20
40	42	48	46	32	28	24	34	38	36	30	26	22
50	44	50	48	34	30	26	36	40	38	32	28	24
60	46	52	50	36	32	28	38	42	40	34	30	26
70	48	54	52	38	34	30	40	44	42	36	32	28
80	50	56	54	40	36	32	42	46	44	38	34	30
90	52	58	56	42	38	34	44	48	46	40	36	32
100	54	59	58	44	40	36	46	50	48	42	38	34

The above table 6.5 illustrates the comparative result analysis of processing time using proposed STFDC-LF technique and GOMOPA technique and SFDC-SOMOPA technique with the existing methods such as Secure-Logging-as-a-Service (SecLaaS) Scheme by Shams Zawoad et al., (2016), Forensic Open-Stack Tools (FROST) by Josiah Dykstra and Alan T. Sherman (2013) and Security as a Service Model by Vijay Varadharajan and Udaya Tupakula (2014). The number of cloud users is considered from 10 to 100 which are taken as input to perform the simulation.

As shown in above table, the performance of analysis of processing time in the proposed methods and existing methods is significantly improved with respect to the number of cloud users. However, the proposed SFDC-SOMOPA technique ensures better results on reducing the processing time than the other methods. The graph is plotted in below figure 6.6 by utilizing the table values from the table 6.5.

The figure 6.6 shows the measurement of processing time by comparing the three proposed techniques as STFDC-LF technique and GOMOPA technique and SFDC-SOMOPA technique with existing methods such as Secure-Logging-as-a-Service (SecLaaS) Scheme, Forensic Open-Stack Tools (FROST) and Security as a Service Model. The above figure clearly describes that the proposed SFDC-SOMOPA technique effectively minimizes the processing time than the other proposed and exiting methods.

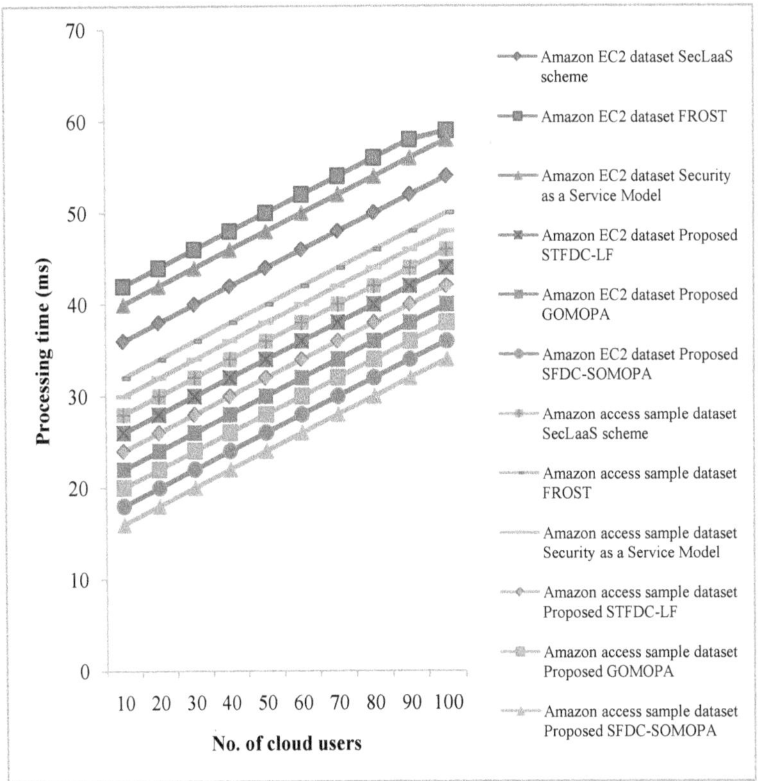

Figure 6.6: Measure of Processing Time

Thus, the forensic investigator significantly carry outs the investigation to identify the malicious user with accurate evidence by implementing the proposed SFDC-SOMOPA technique while transferring the confidential files on government sectors. After separating the cloud log files, the particle swarm optimization approach is carried out to detect the best result as correct evidence of the malicious activities in order to identify the exact malicious user. Here, the fitness function is computed depending on the multi-objective functions as evidence of malicious actions. Based on the fitness value, the, particle is selected for identifying the exact malicious user which has the best fitness value is set as global best evidence. From that, the identification process for discovering exact malicious user, who makes attacks on the confidential data is carried out with the minimal amount of time with the application of proposed SFDC-SOMOPA technique. Moreover, the proposed SFDC-SOMOPA technique reduces the processing time by 33% and 40% when compared to Secure-Logging-as-a-Service (SecLaaS) Scheme by Shams Zawoad et al., (2016), Forensic Open-Stack Tools (FROST) by Josiah Dykstra and Alan T. Sherman (2013) and 37% when compared to Security as a Service Model by Vijay Varadharajan and Udaya Tupakula (2014).

6.3. Summary

The proposed STFDC-LF technique and GOMOPA technique and SFDC-SOMOPA technique are successfully compared with the existing methods such as Secure-Logging-as-a-Service (SecLaaS) Scheme by Shams Zawoad et al., (2016), Forensic Open-Stack Tools (FROST) by Josiah Dykstra and Alan T. Sherman (2013) and % when compared to Security as a Service Model by Vijay Varadharajan and Udaya Tupakula (2014). As illustrated in this research the three proposed method are utilized to identify the malicious user the actual cause for the crime event while transferring files between users and server in the government sectors. At first, the proposed Spatio-temporal Forensic Data Collector and Logging filter (STFDC-LF) technique carries outs the cloud forensic investigation to extract the proof of malicious activities of cloud log files by performing the collection and isolation process. Thus, Gene Optimized Multi-objective Proof Accumulator (GOMOPA) technique identifies the malicious user by submitting the acceptable evidence to the proof accumulator. In addition, Spatiotemporal Forensic Data Collector and Swarm Optimized Multi-Objective Proof Accumulator (SFDC-SOMOPA) technique is proposed to find out the malicious user who initiates the crime with better confidentiality rate by performing privacy preserved forensic investigation on the cloud. Thus, the confidential file transaction is achieved in the government sectors by detecting the malicious user on cloud environment.

CHAPTER VII

CONCLUSION AND FUTURE WORK

7.1. Conclusion

Cloud computing has an enormous attention to deliver cloud services over an internet. During the transmission of confidential data on cloud, providing of security to the cloud data and the privacy of user are the main concern. Some researches were developed for performing the forensic investigation to ensure privacy assured cloud forensic services. However, these developed techniques failed to reduce the time and increase the accuracy and to detect the malicious user on cloud. Thus, Spatio-Temporal Forensic Data Collector and Logging Filter (STFDC-LF) technique, Gene Optimized Multi-objective Proof Accumulator (GOMOPA) technique and Spatiotemporal Forensic Data Collector and Swarm Optimized Multi-Objective Proof Accumulator (SFDC-SOMOPA) technique are proposed to achieve the confidential data transmission within a secured way.

Initially, the proposed Spatio-Temporal Forensic Data Collector and Logging Filter (STFDC-LF) technique is developed with Spatio-Temporal Forensic Data Collector scheme, Event Activity Time Synchronization method and Forensic Logging Filter (FLF) to identify the evidence of malicious activities for particular crime event. At first, various log files from different resources are collected by using Spatio-Temporal Forensic Data Collector scheme. Then, the cloud log files of multiple cloud users are managed at a specific time by introducing an Event Activity Time Synchronization method.

Followed by, the evidences of malicious activities (cloud log files) that are isolated, unrelated to the crime event from collected log files with the help of Forensic Logging Filter (FLF).

Then, Gene Optimized Multi-objective Proof Accumulator (GOMOPA) technique is implemented with gene based approach to detect the malicious user who initiates the crime action on cloud environment. At first, the investigator reports the multi-objective functions such as evidence of the malicious activity, proof of integrity and data possession, provenance information, time stamp information and location information to the proof accumulator. Thus, the evidence of malicious activities as the multi-objective functions of cloud log files are optimized to discover the malicious user with the help of gene based approach by validating the investigated proof with real suspect.

In addition, Spatiotemporal Forensic Data Collector and Swarm Optimized Multi-Objective Proof Accumulator (SFDC-SOMOPA) technique is proposed in order to ensure higher confidentiality rate while performing the cloud services by detecting malicious user on cloud. Initially, the cloud log files of multiple cloud users are acquired related with physical location and the temporal information by using Spatiotemporal Forensic Data Collector. Then, the exact time to identify the evidences of malicious activities is discovered with the aid of Fault tolerant Time Synchronization method.

After that, log files (evidences) of the multiple cloud users which are related or unrelated to the crime event are separated through the Watershed Forensic Logging Filter (WFLF). Finally, evidences with multi objective functions are submitted into proof accumulator using Swarm Optimized Multi-objective Proof Accumulator (SOMOPA). According to the fitness function, the particle swarm optimization find out the exact malicious user who launches the crime action.

Theoretical analysis and experimental results demonstrates that the proposed techniques such as Spatio-Temporal Forensic Data Collector and Logging filter (STFDC-LF) technique, Gene Optimized Multi-objective Proof Accumulator (GOMOPA) technique and Spatiotemporal Forensic Data Collector and Swarm Optimized Multi-Objective Proof Accumulator (SFDC-SOMOPA) technique effectively performs the forensic investigation to detect the malicious user on cloud environment. The experimental evaluation of proposed techniques such as STFDC-LF, GOMOPA and SFDC-SOMOPA technique are conducted by using java language with CloudSim network simulator.

The performance of three proposed techniques is analyzed by using Amazon EC2 dataset and Amazon access sample dataset in the CloudSim network simulator. For conducting simulation, the number of cloud user is taken from 10 to 100 and the number of cloud log files is taken from 5 to 50.

From the experimental results, it is observed that the proposed SFDC-SOMOPA technique uses Amazon access sample dataset to achieve better results in the improvement of investigation accuracy and filtering accuracy up to 27% and 30% by using Spatiotemporal Forensic Data Collector and Watershed Forensic Logging Filter (WFLF) while performing the investigation to detect the malicious user on cloud. Similarly, the confidentiality rate is improved up to 28% by introducing the Swarm Optimized Multi-objective Proof Accumulator (SOMOPA) in the SFDC-SOMOPA technique with Amazon access sample dataset when compared to other proposed and existing methods.

In addition, during the forensic investigation, the Amazon access sample dataset is used in the SFDC-SOMOPA technique to minimize the investigation time and processing time by 49% and 37 % through the performance of Fault tolerant time synchronization and particle swarm optimization than the other proposed and existing methods.

7.2. Limitations and Future Work

The proposed STFDC-LF, GOMOPA and SFDC-SOMOPA techniques are implemented to achieve the secured cloud services with higher confidentiality rate. Then, the cloud forensic investigation is performed in proposed SFDC-SOMOPA technique to carry out the confidential data transmission by identifying the malicious user on cloud. However, the proposed techniques are not developed for recognizing the resource utilization to perform an effective investigation in cloud environment. Although our research work detects the malicious users (attacks) on cloud, the forensic investigator couldn't specify the attack types.

Future analysis is concentrated on overcoming the proposed limitations which are discussed previously. The future direction of proposed works may focus on identifying the resource utilization for ensuring secured cloud services. In future, efficient mechanisms are introduced to find out the different kinds of attacks presented in cloud environment.

References

[1] Adeela Waqar, AsadRaza , HaiderAbbas, Muhammad Khurram Khan, "A framework for preservation of cloud users' data privacy using dynamic Reconstruction of metadata", Journal of Network and Computer Applications, Elsevier, Volume 36, Issue No.1 January 2013, Pages 235–248.

[2] Agreeka Saxena, Gulshan Shrivastava, Kavita Sharma, "Forensic Investigation in Cloud Computing Environment", International Journal of Forensic Computer Science, Volume 2, 2012, Pages 64-74

[3] Ameer Pichan, Mihai Lazarescu and Sie Teng Soh, "Cloud forensics: Technical challenges, solutions and comparative analysis", Digital Investigation, Elsevier, Volume 13, June 2015, Pages 38-57.

[4] Ben Martini and Kim-Kwang Raymond Choo, "An integrated conceptual digital forensic framework for cloud computing," Digital Investigation, Elsevier, Volume 9, Issue No. 2, November 2012, Pages 71–80.

[5] Chen Long and Zhang Qing, "Forensic Analysis to China's Cloud Storage Services", International Journal of Machine Learning and Computing, Volume 5, Issue No.6, December 2015, Pages 467-470.

[6] Chi Yang, Xuyun Zhang, Changmin Zhong ,Chang Liu ,Jian Pei, Kotagiri Ramamohanarao, Jinjun Chen, "A spatio temporal compression based approach for efficient big data processing on Cloud", Journal of Computer and System Sciences, Elsevier, Volume 80, Issue No.8, December 2014, Pages 1563–1583.

[7] Christian J. D'Orazio and Kim-Kwang Raymond Choo, "Circumventing iOS Security Mechanisms for APT Forensic Investigations: A Security Taxonomy for Cloud Apps", Future Generation Computer Systems, Elsevier, November 2016, Pages 1-24.

[8] Christopher Stelly and Vassil Roussev, "SCARF: A container-based approach to cloud-scale digital forensic processing", Digital Investigation, Elsevier, Volume 22, Supplement, August 2017, Pages 39-47.

[9] Chu-Hsing Lin, Chen-Yu Lee and Tang-Wei Wu, "A Cloud-aided RSA Signature Scheme for Sealing and Storing the Digital Evidences in Computer Forensics", International Journal of Security and Its Applications, Volume 6, Issue No. 2, April 2012, Pages 241-244.

[10] Daniel Spiekermann, Jorg Keller and Tobias Eggendorfer,"Network forensic investigation in OpenFlow networks with ForCon", Digital Investigation, Elsevier, Volume 20, Supplement, March 2017, Pages 66-74.

[11] Darren Quick and Kim-Kwang Raymond Choo, "Forensic collection of cloud storage data: Does the act of collection result in changes to the data or its metadata?", Digital Investigation, Elsevier, Volume 10, Issue No.3, October 2013, Pages 266-277.

[12] Deevi Radha Rani, Sk. Nazma Sultana and Pasala Lourdu Sravani, "Challenges of Digital Forensics in Cloud Computing Environment", Indian Journal of Science and Technology, Volume 9, Issue No.17, May 2016, Pages 1-7.

[13] Deoyani Shirkhedkar and Sulabha Patil, "Analysis of Various Digital Forensic Techniques for Cloud Computing", International Journal of Advanced Research in Computer Science, Volume 5, Issue No.4, April 2014, Pages 104-107.

[14] Doowon Jeong, Jungheum Park, Sangjin Lee, and Chulhoon Kang, "Investigation Methodology of a Virtual Desktop Infrastructure for IoT", Journal of Applied Mathematics, Hindawi Publishing Corporation, Volume 2015, July 2014, Pages 1-10.

[15] Dr Mark Taylor, Dr John Haggerty, David Gresty, Peter Almond and Dr Tom Berry, "Forensic investigation of social networking applications" , Network Security, Elsevier, Volume 2014, Issue No.11, November 2014, Pages 9-16.

[16] Ezz El-Din Hemdan and Manjaiah D.H, "Forensic Analysis Approach Based on Metadata and Hash Values for Digital Objects in the Cloud", International Journal of Innovative

Research in Computer and Communication Engineering, Volume 3, Issue No. 7, October 2015, Pages 1-6.

[17] Farhood Norouzizadeh Dezfoli, Ali Dehghantanha, Ramlan Mahmoud, Nor Fazlida Binti Mohd Sani and Farid Daryabar, "Digital Forensic Trends and Future", International Journal of Cyber-Security and Digital Forensics (IJCSDF), Volume 2, Issue No. 2, 2013, Pages 48-76.

[18] Flavio Cruz, Andreas Moser, Michael Cohen,"A scalable file based data store for forensic analysis", Digital Investigation, Elsevier, Volume 12, Supplement 1, March 2015, Pages 90-101.

[19] Frank M. Gotz, "Genolab-Forensic biostatistics with cloud computing", Forensic Science International: Genetics Supplement Series, Elsevier, Volume 5, December 2015, Pages 438-440.

[20] G.Geethakumari and AbhaBelorkar, "Regenerating Cloud Attack Scenarios using LVM2 based System Snapshots for Forensic Analysis", International Journal of Cloud Computing and Services Science (IJ-CLOSER), Volume 1, Issue No.3, August 2012, Pages 134-141.

[21] GAO Yuanzhao and LI Binglong, "A Forensic Method for Efficient File Extraction in HDFS Based on Three-Level Mapping", Wuhan University, Journal of Natural Sciences, Volume 22, Issue No.2, 2017, Pages 114-126.

[22] Ghania Al Sadi, "Cloud Computing Architecture and Forensic Investigation Challenges", International Journal of Computer Applications, Volume 124, Issue No. 7, August 2015, Pages 20-25.

[23] Hamisu Alhaji Ali, "Cloud Computing Security: An Investigation into the Security Issues and Challenges Associated with Cloud Computing, for both Data Storage and Virtual Applications", International Research Journal of Electronics & Computer Engineering Volume 1, Issue No.2, July-September 2015, Pages 15-20.

[24] Himanshu Nimje and Dr K. N. Honwadkar, "Digital Forensic Investigation and Analysis of Android Mobile", International Journal of Science and Research (IJSR), Volume 4, Issue No.12, December 2015, Pages 704-707.

[25] Hui Tian, Zhaoyi Chen, Chin-Chen Chang, Minoru Kuribayashi, Yongfeng Huang, Yiqiao Cai, Yonghong Chen and Tian Wang, "Enabling public auditability for operation behaviors in cloud storage", Soft Computing, Springer, April 2017, Volume 21, Issue No.8, Pages 2175–2187.

[26] Hyunji Chung, Jungheum Park, Sangjin Lee and Cheulhoon Kang, "Digital forensic investigation of cloud storage services", Digital Investigation, Elsevier, Volume 9, Issue No. 2, November 2012, Pages 81-95.

[27] Hyun-Woo Kim, Gangman Yi, Jong Hyuk Park and Young-Sik Jeong, "Adaptive resource management using many-core processing for fault tolerance based on cyber-physical cloud systems", Future Generation Computer Systems, Elsevier, July 2017, Pages 1-22.

[28] Jasbir Kaur and Supriya Kinger, "Efficient Algorithm for Fault Tolerance in Cloud Computing", International Journal of Computer Science and Information Technologies, Volume 5, Issue No. 5, 2014, Pages 6278-6281.

[29] Jason S.Hale, "Amazon Cloud Drive forensic analysis", Digital Investigation, Elsevier, Volume 10, Issue No.3, October 2013, Pages 259-265.

[30] Jian Shen, Jun Shen , Xiaofeng Chen , Xinyi Huang , Willy Susilo, "An Efficient Public Auditing Protocol with Novel Dynamic Structure for Cloud Data", IEEE Transactions on Information Forensics and Security , Volume 12, Issue No.10, October 2017, Pages 2402 - 2415.

[31] Jiawei Yuan and Shucheng Yu, "Public integrity auditing for dynamic data sharing with multiuser modification," IEEE Transactions on Information Forensics and Security , Volume 10, Issue No.8, August 2015, Pages 1717–1726.

[32] Jin Li, Xiaofeng Chenb, Qiong Huangc, Duncan S. Wongd, "Digital provenance: Enabling secure data forensics in cloud computing", Future Generation Computer Systems, Elsevier, Volume 37, July 2014, Pages 259–266.

[33] Josiah Dykstra and Alan T. Sherman, "Acquiring forensic evidence from infrastructure-as-a-service cloud computing: Exploring and evaluating tools, trust, and techniques" Digital Investigation, Elsevier, Volume 9, August 2012, Pages 90–98.

[34] Josiah Dykstra and Alan T. Sherman, "Design and implementation of FROST: digital forensic tools for the open stack cloud computing platform", Digital Investigation, Elsevier, Volume 10, Supplement, August 2013, Pages 87-95.

[35] Keyun Ruan, Joe Carthy, Tahar Kechadi, Ibrahim Baggili, "Cloud forensics definitions and critical criteria for cloud forensic capability: an overview of survey result", Digital Investigation, Elsevier, Volume 10, Issue No.1, June 2013, Pages 34–43.

[36] M. Edington Alex and R. Kishore, "Forensics framework for cloud computing", Computers & Electrical Engineering, Elsevier, Volume 60, May 2017, Pages 193-205.

[37] M. Taylor, J.Haggerty, D.Gresty and R.Hegarty, "Digital evidence in cloud computing systems", Computer Law & Security Review, Elsevier, Volume 26, Issue No. 3, May 2010, Pages 304-308.

[38] Mahmoud M. Nasreldin, Magdy El-Hennawy, Heba K. Aslan, and Adel El-Hennaw, "Digital Forensics Evidence Acquisition and Chain of Custody in Cloud Computing", International Journal of Computer Science Issues, Volume 12, Issue No.1, January 2015, Pages 153-160.

[39] Mark Taylor, John Haggerty, David Gresty and David Lamb, "Forensic investigation of cloud computing systems", Network Security, Elsevier, Volume 2011, Issue No. 3, March 2011, Pages 4-10.

[40] Meng You, Luan Zhongzhi, Qian Depei, "Differentiating data collection for cloud environment monitoring", China Communications, Volume 11, Issue No. 4, April 2014, Pages 13 - 24.

[41] Ming Sang Chang, "Forensic investigation of Amazon Cloud Drive on Windows 10", IJISET - International Journal of Innovative Science, Engineering & Technology, Volume 3 Issue No.6, June 2016, Pages 478- 482.

[42] Muhammad Imran, Helmut Hlavacs, Inam Ul Haq, Bilal Jan,Fakhri Alam Khan and Awais Ahmad, "Provenance based data integrity checking and verification in cloud environments", PLoS ONE, Volume 12, Issue No.5, May 2017, Pages 1-19.

[43] Muhammad Irfan, Haider Abbas, Yunchuan Sun, Anam Sajid and Maruf Pasha, "A framework for cloud forensics evidence collection and analysis using security information and event management", Security and Communication Networks, Volume 9, Issue No.16, November 2016, Pages 3790–3807.

[44] Muhammad Naeem Ahmed Khan and ShahWali Ullah, "A log aggregation forensic analysis framework for cloud computing environments", Computer Fraud & Security, Elsevier, Volume 2017, Issue No.7, July 2017, Pages 11-16.

[45] Niken Dwi Wahyu Cahyani, Nurul Hidayah Ab Rahman, William Bradley Glisson and Kim-Kwang Raymond Choo, "The Role of Mobile Forensics in Terrorism Investigations Involving the Use of Cloud Storage Service and Communication Apps", Mobile Networks and Applications, Springer, April 2017, Volume 22, Issue No. 2, Pages 240–254.

[46] Nithya Chidambaram, Pethuru Raj, K. Thenmozhi and Rengarajan Amirtharajan, "Enhancing the Security of Customer Data in Cloud Environments Using a Novel Digital Fingerprinting Technique", Hindawi Publishing Corporation, International Journal of Digital Multimedia Broadcasting, Volume 2016, 2016, Pages 1-6.

[47] Pranay Chauhan and PratoshBansal, "Emphasizing on Various Security Issues in Cloud Forensic Framework", Indian Journal of Science and Technology", Volume 10, Issue No. 18, May 2017, Pages 1-7.

[48] Prasad Purnaye and Varshapriya Jyotinagar, "Cloud forensics:Volatile data preservation", International Journal of Computer Science Engineering (IJCSE), Volume 4, Issue No.2, March 2015, Pages 41-43.

[49] Quang Do, Ben Martini and Kim-Kwang Raymond Choo, "A Cloud-Focused Mobile Forensics Methodology", IEEE Cloud Computing, Volume 2, Issue No. 4, July-August 2015, Pages 60-65.

[50] R.B. van Baar, H.M.A. van Beek, E.J. van Eijk, "Digital Forensics as a Service: A game changer", Digital Investigation, Elsevier, Digital Investigation, Elsevier, Volume 11, Supplement 1, May 2014, Pages 54-62.

[51] Rameshwari Malik and Pramod Kumar, " A novel Approach for Intrusion Detection and Prevention Technique for Cloud based on FVM Approach", International journal pf Computer Applications, Volume 118, Issue No.1, May 2015, Pages 20-24.

[52] Raymond Lutui, "A multidisciplinary digital forensic investigation process model", Business Horizons, Elsevier, Volume 59, Issue No.6, March-April 2016, Pages 593-604.

[53] Roberto Battistoni, Roberto DiPietro and Flavio Lombardi, "CURE—Towards enforcing a reliable timeline for cloud forensics: Model, architecture, and experiments", Computer Communications, Elsevier, Volumes 91–92, October 2016, Pages 29-43.

[54] Rohini Patil, SuchetaKudake, PornimaJathade, Pallavi Kale and Prof. PankajAgarkar, "MobSafe: Forensic Analysis For Android Applications Using Cloud Stack And Data Mining", International Journal of Advanced Research in Computer Engineering & Technology (IJARCET), Volume 5, Issue No.4, April 2016, Pages 1111-1116.

[55] Saad Alqahtany, Nathan Clarke, Steven Furnell and Christoph Reich,"A forensic acquisition and analysis system for IaaS", Cluster Computing, Springer, Volume 19, Issue No. 1, March 2016, Pages 439–453.

[56] Sandra Zancajo-Blazquez, Susana Lagüela-López, Diego González-Aguilera and Joaquín Martínez-Sánchez, "Segmentation of Indoor Mapping Point Clouds Applied to Crime Scenes Reconstruction", IEEE Transactions On Information Forensics And Security, Volume 10, Issue No. 7, July 2015, Pages 1350- 1358.

[57] Sarah F. Bailey, Melissa K. Scheible, Christopher Williams, Deborah S.B.S Silva, Marina Hoggan, Christopher Eichman, and Seth A. Faith, "Secure and Robust Cloud Computing for High-throughput Forensic Microsatellite Sequence Analysis and Databasing", Forensic Science International: Genetics, Elsevier, Volume 31, November 2017, Pages 40-47.

[58] Sean Thorpe and Indrajit Ray, "Detecting temporal inconsistency in virtual machine activity timelines", Journal of Information Assurance and Security (JIAS), Volume 7, Issue No.1, 2012, Pages 21-34.

[59] Shahaf Rozanski and Cellebrite,"Using cloud data to accelerate forensic investigations", Network Security, Elsevier, Volume 2015, Issue No. 9, September 2015, Pages 19-20.

[60] Shams Zawoad, Amit Kumar Dutta ,Ragib Hasan, "Towards Building Forensics Enabled Cloud Through Secure Logging-as-a-Service", IEEE Transactions on Dependable and Secure Computing ,Volume 13, Issue No. 2, March-April 2016 , Pages 148 – 162.

[61] Sonal Saokar, Sulabha Patil and Rajiv Dharaskar, "Design Framework of Digital Forensic for Cloud Computing: A Review", International Journal of Advanced Computational Engineering and Networking, Volume 3, Issue No.12, December 2015, Pages 91-93.

[62] Suchana Datta, Koushik Majumder and Debashis D, "Review on Cloud Forensics: An Open Discussion on Challenges and Capabilities", International Journal of Computer Applications, Volume 145, Issue No.1, July 2016, Pages 1-8.

[63] Suleman Khan, Abdullah Gani , Ainuddin Wahid, Abdul Wahab, Mustapha Aminu Bagiwa, Muhammad Shiraz, Samee U. Khan, Rajkumar Buyya And Albert Y. Zomaya,, "Cloud Log Forensics: Foundations, State of the Art, and Future Directions", ACM Computing Surveys (CSUR), Volume 49, Issue No. 1, May 2016, Pages 1-44.

[64] Suleman Khan, Abdullah Gani, Ainuddin Wahid Abdul Wahab, Salman Iqbal, Ahmed Abdelaziz, Omar Adil Mahdi, Abdelmuttlib Ibrahim Abdallaahmed, Muhammad Shiraz, Yusor Rafid Bahar Al-Mayouf, Ziar Khan, Kwangman Ko, Muhammad Khurram Khan, and Victor Chan, "Towards an Applicability of Current Network Forensics for Cloud Networks: A SWOT Analysis", IEEE Access , Volume 4, December 2016, Pages 9800 – 9820.

[65] Suleman Khan, Muhammad Shiraz, AinuddinWahid AbdulWahab, Abdullah Gani, Qi Han and Zulkanain Bin Abdul Rahman, "A Comprehensive Review on Adaptability of Network Forensics Frameworks for Mobile Cloud Computing", Hindawi Publishing Corporation, The Scientific World Journal, Volume 2014, 2014, Pages 1-27.

[66] Vassil Roussev and Shane McCulley,"Forensic analysis of cloud-native artifacts", Digital Investigation, Elsevier, Volume 16, Supplement, March 2016, Pages 104-113.

[67] Vijay Varadharajan and Udaya Tupakula, "Security as a Service Model for Cloud Environment", IEEE Transactions on Network and Service Management, Volume 11, Issue No. 1, March 2014, Pages 60 – 75.

[68] Yee-Yang Teing, Ali Dehghantanha and Kim-Kwang Raymond Choo, "CloudMe forensics: A case of big data forensic investigation", Wiley Publications, July 2017, Pages 1-12.

[69] Yee-Yang Teing, Ali Dehghantanha, Kim-Kwang Raymond Choo, Tooska Dargahi, and Mauro Conti, "Forensic Investigation of Cooperative Storage Cloud Service: Symform as a Case Study", Volume 62, Issue No.3, May 2017, Pages 641-654.

[70] Yong Yu, Yannan Li, Jianbing Ni, Guomin Yang, Yi Mu and Willy Susilo, "Comments on Public Integrity Auditing for Dynamic Data Sharing with Multi-user Modification", IEEE Transactions on Information Forensics and Security , Volume 11, Issue No. 3, March 2016, Pages 658 – 659.

[71] Zhen Chen, Fuye Han, Junwei Cao , Xin Jiang, Shuo Chen, "Cloud computing-based forensic analysis for collaborative network security management system", Tsinghua Science and Technology, Volume, 18, Issue No. 1, February 2013, Pages 40 – 50.

[72] Zhen Xu, Cong Wang, Kui Ren, Lingyu Wang, Bingsheng Zhang, "Proof-Carrying Cloud Computation: The Case of Convex Optimization", IEEE Transactions on Information Forensics and Security, Volume 9, Issue No. 11, November 2014, Pages 1790 – 1803.

[73] Zhengwei Qi, Chengcheng Xiang, Ruhui Ma, Jian Li, Haibing Guan and David S. L. Wei, "ForenVisor: A Tool for Acquiring and Preserving Reliable Data in Cloud Live Forensics", IEEE Transactions on Cloud Computing, Volume 5, Issue No. 3, July-September 2017, Pages 1-14.

www.ingramcontent.com/pod-product-compliance
Lightning Source LLC
LaVergne TN
LVHW082346171026
850499LV00040B/1345
* 9 7 8 9 3 8 7 8 6 2 7 8 4 *

CLOUD SECURITY - Spatiotemporal Forensic Data Analysis

Dr. Sripriya Arunachalam M.C.A, M.Phil., Ph.D

Dr. M. Sundara Rajan M.Sc., M.Phil., Ph.D

Published by

BONFRING®
Intellectual Integrity

CLOUD SECURITY - Spatiotemporal Forensic Data Analysis

9 789387 862784 >

ISBN 978-93-87862-78-4

Authors

Dr. Sripriya Arunachalam M.C.A, M.Phil., Ph.D

Dr. M. Sundara Rajan M.Sc., M.Phil., Ph.D

Bonfring

309, 2nd Floor,

5th Street Extension, Gandhipuram,

Coimbatore-641 012.

Tamilnadu, India.

E-mail: info@bonfring.org

Website: www.bonfring.org

Phone: 0422 4213231